INTRODUCTION TO LAW AND LEGAL THINKING

by Anthony D'Amato

Leighton Professor of Law

Northwestern University

Transnational Publishers, Inc.
Irvington-on-Hudson, New York

Library of Congress-in-Publication Data

D'Amato, Anthony A.
Introduction to law and legal thinking / by Anthony D'Amato.
p. cm.
Rev. ed. of: How to understand the law. c1989.
Includes bibliographical references and index.
ISBN 1-57105-015-9
1. Law—United States. 2. Law—Philisophy. I. D'Amato, Anthony A. How to understand the law. II. Title.
KF380.C35 1996
349.73—dc20
[347.3] 95-53030
CIP

CONTENTS

INTRODUCTION

An undergraduate studying political theory or political science wants to know more than just the role of the judicial system as a branch of government—he or she wants to become acquainted with the intellectual perspective of law. A foreign student coming to this country to spend a year or more in law school wants to have a preview of the underlying philosophy of American law. A student who is thinking seriously about going to law school already knows a great deal about the legal profession. But what about law itself—what kinds of "legal thinking" lie ahead?

The book you are holding is perhaps the only reader-friendly book available today that deals with the deep and basic concepts of law in general, and American law in particular. But it doesn't simply introduce the concepts; rather, it is an introduction to thinking about the concepts.

I've taught law at Northwestern for over a quarter of a century (it doesn't seem that long). The subjects I've taught have been wide-ranging: constitutional law, environmental law, legal ethics, jurisprudence, torts, and international law. In each class I have learned a great deal from my students, perhaps more than they learned from me. In addition to teaching, I have been an active litigator involving matters of human rights. I have litigated cases against governments, including Saudi Arabia, the former Soviet Union, Mexico, Austria, and the United States (the latter back in the 1960s and 1970s when I took up cases that challenged the constitutionality of the Vietnam War). I was the first American lawyer to argue a case in the European Court of Human Rights in Strasbourg. My courtroom experience has,

I believe, substantially helped my research and teaching. I believe in practicing what one teaches.

If you are thinking about going to law school and becoming a lawyer, this book may help you in making your career decision. If you like the kind of reasoning in this book, if you enjoy the concepts and the way I've tried to illustrate them whenever possible by real-life examples, and if you enjoy the advocate's perspective that I've utilized in writing the book, then I think there's a good chance that you will enjoy the study of law. Lawyers never cease studying the law, never stop keeping up with the latest decisions and developments. Whatever career you choose, it should be something that you really enjoy doing every single day of your life.

A first-year student at Harvard Law School went home for the Thanksgiving recess and his parents started carrying on about how proud they were that he was a law student. His aunt, attempting to be polite, said, "So tell me, how many laws have you learned so far?"

Now, that was a law joke. It is distinctly unfunny to anyone except lawyers. Lawyers are amused because they recognize the sheer inappropriateness of the aunt's question. For not only has the Harvard student not yet learned any laws, but in all probability he won't learn any laws during the remainder of his three years of law school.

Lawyers don't need to know laws; they only need to know how to look them up. Law school training enables a lawyer to figure out which laws to look up and how to look them up, and most importantly, what on earth to do with them once they are found.

A superior law school education, therefore, is education in the concepts of law, the generalities of law, the groundwork of the legal system upon which one can, at any later time, locate and make sense out of rules, regulations, statutes, and cases. This book is an introduction to a superior law school education.

CHAPTER 1. WHAT LAW DOES

A. THE FUNCTION OF LAW

Here is a simple definition of the function of law: *law is an artificial mechanism designed to channel human behavior into the directions society wants.* The "mechanism" consists of words and other signs and symbols that contain the language of the law, together with a whole setup of authoritative interpreters and appliers of the law (such as courts and judges), accompanied by enforcers of the law (such as police and a prison system). The words, symbols and signs are what we normally call the "law" itself; the other mechanisms apply and enforce the law. You may have noticed that I've omitted a mechanism for creating or modifying the law, such as a legislature. While law-creating mechanisms are typically part of modern legal systems, they were not always thought necessary. In medieval times, judges simply applied law that they said was immutable and immemorial; it was always around, never created and never destroyed. "The mind of man runneth not to the contrary," they said of the origins of this omnipresent law. Of course we can nowadays be skeptical and say that any rule of law must have originated somewhere, and if we are legal realists we will indeed take that position. But it's perfectly consistent to imagine law functioning in a society where the rules don't change and no one knows or remembers how they got started. Later in this book we will review how the three major schools of legal thought—positivism, realism, and natural law—have conceived of the problem of where the law comes from.

But for now, let us look at what law does. The definition I gave in the previous paragraph emphasizes the deliberate channeling function of law. It acknowledges that the only reason for having law at all is that it influences human behavior. Legal rules would be utterly worthless if they totally failed to influence anyone's behavior. To be sure, one might argue that even if law doesn't influence behavior, nevertheless as long as people behave in relatively consistent and generalizable ways, there is a kind of "law"—a law that generally describes their behavior. We might describe this as a kind of sociological rule. But there's a difference between the sociological rule that most Americans watch television on Monday nights and saying that there is a law requiring it. The "law" that I deal with in this book is that which the average person asks about in the question: "what *must I do or avoid doing,* in order to stay within the law?"

As this question indicates, law channels our behavior in many ways other than the simple one of telling us to refrain from doing certain things, such as laws prohibiting the robbing of banks or driving through a red traffic signal light. Some laws require us to act, such as the requirement that we pay taxes on our income. You cannot be law-abiding by minding your own business and doing nothing; if you do nothing, you will be prosecuted for failing to file income-tax returns. Even so, for the most part law tells us what we should *not* do.

But there is a kind of law different from prohibitions and prescriptions. Although not readily thought of as "law" by the average person, there are rules of law that come to us in the form of conditional statements. They *empower* us to do certain things without requiring us to do them. For instance, there is a conditional license law; it says that if we would like to drive a car, we have to obtain a license. The license law is not a prescription—it does not say that we must drive a car. Nor is it a blanket prohibition—it does not forbid the driving of cars. Rather, it empowers us to drive a car so long as we obtain a license. Another example of a conditional law that empowers us, this one not involving a licensing procedure, is the law of wills: you don't have to leave a will, but if you want to have a valid will that succeeds in transferring your property after you die, you have to execute the will in a certain way, with witnesses and so on, according to the specific rules in your jurisdiction. Indeed, all the laws of contract and sales are of this conditional form. You don't have to enter into a contract, but if you want to, you have to do it a certain way if you want the legal system to enforce the contract in the event that the other party reneges on his or her obligation to you. We say that license laws, the laws of wills, and the contract laws, give us legal powers. They enable us to change legal relationships by simply choosing to enter into certain kinds of activities, such as making a will or a contract. They empower us to do these things without requiring us either to do them or to refrain from doing them.

Here's a little mental exercise. We've seen that laws come in the form of prohibitions, prescriptions, and powers. Can we reduce these categories into one category? The legal philosopher Hans Kelsen thought of a way. He reasoned as follows: an individual is free to do anything. But some things that an individual chooses to do will be costly. In particular, the law imposes certain costs upon certain choices that individuals might make. Thus if you want to rob a bank, you are free to do so, but the law will impose a cost upon you. The law will put you in prison for a specified period of time (say, five years). Hence we can reformulate the no-robbery prohibition in terms of a power: "if you choose to rob a bank, then the law will imprison you for five years." We can reformulate the tax law as follows: "if you choose to not file a tax return, the law will imprison you for three years." In this fashion, all prohibitions and prescriptions can be transformed into powers.

Kelsen's idea seems a bit stilted; he is forcing prohibitions and prescriptions into the strange form of an empowering statement. He later refined and improved his reasoning by changing the person to whom the law is addressed, as we shall see in Chapter 3. But for the moment, Kelsen's idea does highlight the voluntaristic aspect of law. It points out the fact that the law simply adds a cost—often an intolerably high cost—to alternatives that we can freely choose. We are then led to ask whether law is indeed based upon the fundamental assumption of human free will.

B. OBJECTIVE LAW AND THE QUESTION OF FREE WILL

Contrary to the implications of Kelsen's position, I will now contend that law can more efficiently be studied as an objective and not as a subjective phenomenon. I will try to show that there is a conceptual attractiveness in explaining law mechanistically—as if it does not depend on the free will of human beings. Indeed, I argue that law is more understandable if we do not presuppose a mind or a will that the law acts upon.

We will lose something, however, if we regard law as a mechanism. We will lose the "justice" component of the law. I want to come back to "justice" in Chapter 7 of this book. But for now, our purpose is to get an efficient overview of law. Accordingly, I will now take a mechanistic, deterministic, and objective approach to our subject.

Here is a demonstration of how "law" can work even if we assume that human beings have no free will. Let us take one of the simplest of all legal rules—the ordinary traffic signal. It is a legal rule addressed to drivers of vehicles that simply means "stop on red, go on green." It is easy for us to assume that all drivers have the free will whether to obey the traffic signal or run the lights—as they say in England, "shoot the lights." But now suppose we have a totally impartial observer, an extraterrestrial visitor from another galaxy who observes traffic patterns at a busy intersection in the loop in Chicago. Our visitor duly observes that when the red beam shines from the stationary light at the corner of the intersection, it causes the wheeled vehicles to come to a stop; conversely, the green beam appears to energize those vehicles, setting them in motion. Our careful visitor notices that inside the hard metallic vehicles are "soft" machines who inhabit the vehicles and make gestures at a control panel and spin a primitive wheel. Perhaps the red and green beams from the traffic signal stimulate these soft machines who in turn direct the operation of the hard machines. Or perhaps the hard machines determine the responses of the soft machines. Regardless of which controls what, the important observation that the ET visitor makes is that the light beams affect the behavior of the vehicles.

If the ET visitor observes the situation for a period of time, once in a while a red beam will be observed to fail to stop a car. The visitor will probably conclude that the car has a defective beam-detection mechanism. But this is not unusual; on such a primitive planet, one could hardly expect its machines to operate perfectly.

Note that no assumptions are needed about free will. From the ET visitor's point of view, everything is explained mechanistically. While *we*—the soft machines inside the automobiles—*think* that we are making choices, what we think may simply be a form of self delusion. It may be the action of our cerebral cortexes attempting to rationalize to our minds the deterministic behavior of our bodies. But this is not a book about the philosophy of the mind-body problem or the basis of epistemology, so we need look no further at the question of what "really" is going on inside our minds. My point is that the external perspective—which I have characterized in the traffic example as the ET visitor's perspective—may be the most efficient and revealing way to understand the workings of the law.[1]

Thus, I have invoked the extraterrestrial visitor to argue that a legal rule, such as a traffic signal, works even if we are machines lacking in free will. Machines can react to signals in their environment. The next step is to notice that there is nothing intrinsic about a red or green beam in my sci-fi example that made the cars stop at the intersection. Ordinary words have the same signalling power. The words "keep off the grass" will inform a person that unpleasant consequences, such as being stopped by the police, might attend walking across the grass. The words, then, are a signal to the mind, and our bodies respond the same way we do to many environmental signals. The words or the signal act as stimuli, and with the intervention of our minds as a translating device, our bodies respond. So far, no free will is needed.

It is certainly clear that words can affect our behavior. When the words of the law tell us to do something or refrain from doing something, we react to those words. The words signal to us that unless we do thus-and-so, certain unpleasant consequences are likely to befall us. Thus, if a legislature enacts a law decreasing the speed limit from 65 to 55 on a certain highway, many of the drivers using that highway will change their behavior and reduce their speed, for the words of the sign "Speed Limit 55" signals to the drivers that the unpleasant consequence of being arrested for speeding will result if they do not reduce their speed. Not all of the drivers will reduce their speed, but many of them will—all by a very inexpensive change in one of the signals in our environment. Tentatively, therefore, I conclude that even if you and I had no free

[1] This "objective" perspective was first brilliantly depicted by Judge Oliver Wendell Holmes. See Bibliography.

will, no power to do anything other than what we in fact do, the law would be exactly what it is now. For what we do is a function of all the sensory inputs we receive, and the "speed limit" sign is one of those sensory inputs.

My further contention is that this mechanistic view of law helps us, at the beginning, to understand law better. Later on, in Chapter 7, I will cut back on this mechanistic picture when I discuss the function of justice.

C. THEORIES OF CRIMINAL PENALTY

To see if a mechanistic conception of law can be sustained, we should apply it to the area of law where common sense tells us it is the least likely to work, namely, criminal law. Isn't criminal law predicated on the notion of punishment—that a person who commits a crime is morally blameworthy and deserving of punishment? If people lack free will, how can we blame them for what they do? And wouldn't it be immoral—or at least grossly inconsistent—for us to punish people for doing things that they could not have avoided doing because they lacked free will? Hence, criminal law is the hardest test for the mechanistic theory of law. Let's see if it passes the test.

Taking the hardest example within criminal law, let us consider Mr. X, a man who is born with defective genes—genes that induce him toward criminal behavior. How does the law justify "punishing" this man for crimes that he has committed?

I put the term "punishing" in quotes because I want to argue that it begs the question. It is clear that we cannot ever justify punishing someone for something he could not have avoided doing. We don't hit our dishwasher if it malfunctions, we don't kick our vacuum cleaner if the rubber band in it snaps, and we don't scold our word processor if it loses the last half hour's worth of manuscript that we have programmed. (Of course, some people might do these things, but we consider their behavior aberrant or in some cases funny—as when the Three Stooges or Laurel and Hardy yell at the tools they use.)

So, if we cannot justify "punishing" Mr. X for committing a crime, we have to inquire whether the term "punishing" is an appropriate description for putting him in prison. The way to begin to unravel this question is to ask *why* we imprison the man.

1. Punishment

If our answer is, "to punish him," then I think we can all agree that we cannot justify what we do. But we may have other answers. Indeed, I think a mechanistic view of law can provide us with some fairly satisfactory answers. As to each of the following answers, you should ask yourself whether you are completely or partially satisfied that the answer explains society's decision to imprison Mr. X, the man with defective genes.

2. Deterrence

Instead of "punishment" as a reason, consider the theory of deterrence. We imprison Mr. X for ten years in order to deter the crime of armed robbery. Note that the deterrence theory does not apply to Mr. X himself. It applies to everyone but Mr. X. He isn't deterred from committing the crime, and in fact, because he committed it, we know for sure that he was not deterred. Even if he knew when he committed it that he would be penalized ten years, he was not in fact deterred. So, the theory of deterrence can not apply to Mr. X. We are imprisoning Mr. X solely as an example to others! Since Mr. X is just an example, it doesn't matter whether he has free will. Free will or not, he goes to prison so as to deter others from committing the crime that he committed.

As for all the other people out there—the ones being deterred by our imprisoning Mr. X—they don't have to have free will to be deterred, as we saw in the traffic-light example. Rather, deterrence works because their minds switch off a possible course of action so as to avoid the pain of imprisonment.

You might object to the deterrence theory by pointing out that among the people out there whom we are trying to deter is Mr. Y, who has defective genes similar to those of Mr. X, and who will not be deterred by the fact that X has been imprisoned for ten years. Indeed, you could add the fact that Mr. X himself was not deterred, even though he obviously knew that other people before him who were convicted of armed robbery received long prison sentences. So isn't this a hole in the deterrence theory?

Advocates of the deterrence theory can reply in two ways. First, they can say that they never claim that deterrence is 100% effective. We know that people commit crimes every day and many are caught and convicted; obviously deterrence doesn't work in all cases. But it works in a sufficient number of cases so that the crime statistics are a lot lower than they would be if criminals were not imprisoned. It is like the traffic light example; not every car stopped at the red light, but most of them did. Secondly, advocates of the deterrence theory can say that we are not really sure even about Mr. X and Mr. Y. Did Mr. X in fact commit armed robbery in broad daylight when there were police nearby? Probably not. Most crimes are committed in circumstances where there are relatively few people around, and not in sight of the police. This suggests that the typical criminal, including X, looks for situations where he can "get away with it," and not be caught. In other words, imprisonment does deter X and Y, in the sense that they are more circumspect about the timing of their nefarious activities. It is certainly true that different people calculate different odds about being apprehended and convicted for their crimes. The very fact that Mr. X tried to reduce the odds of being caught means that he adjusted his behavior slightly in light of the deterrence factor. Most of us adjust our behavior a great deal more—all the way up to the point where we don't commit the crime. Criminals such as X and Y tend to adjust their behavior to the point of committing the crime under the least detectable circumstances. So the deterrence theory may work as far as it goes. What the defective-gene theory should tell us is that increasing the penalty for crime will probably have a negligible effect as far as deterring X and Y are concerned, and that for people like X and Y the best way to reduce crime is to have more police personnel visible on the streets.

But deterrence will not work for some people, regardless of "defective genes," if imprisonment itself is not painful to them. Consider the case of Charles Manson, the Los Angeles "cult killer" who directed the brutal and senseless knife-murders of at least nine persons including actress Sharon Tate when she was pregnant. When Manson was convicted for murder, California did not have the death penalty. Interviews with Manson in prison brought out the fact that he had spent much of his youth behind bars and actually preferred prison life to "life in the real world." Prison to him meant security, routine, not worrying about getting food and shelter, and so forth. It was alleged that although Manson had an extreme fear of dying, and would have been deterred if the law had provided for capital punishment, in fact the thought of mere imprisonment for his crimes was no deterrent; it was an attraction to him. This example, like the others I've given, shows that deterrence theory is built upon empirical assumptions that should be continually tested and retested. I'm personally opposed to capital punishment, but the Manson story is one that I've found very troublesome in light of my opposition.

3. Social Contract

A third theory can be called the "social contract" theory. It is perhaps close to the biblical "eye for an eye and tooth for a tooth" concept. Society says that if you harm a member of society you have to pay for it. You have an implicit contract with society not to violate society's fundamental rules, but if you do, society will fulfill its end of the contract by imprisoning you. Society does this not so much as a penalty but simply to ensure respect for its contracts.

This theory is rather close to the deterrence theory in that society carries out its end of the bargain in order to show to others—not necessarily just to you—that it will carry out its contracts in all cases and imprison all criminals. But it is slightly different from the deterrence theory in that it is a way of institutionalizing vengeance. If we had no legal system at all, we might expect the friends and relatives of the victim of a crime to go after and punish the criminal. "Vigilante justice" is the term used for this process in the old west. But in an organized society with a legal system, society monopolizes the retribution process; the friends and relatives will be placated because they know that society will catch, accuse, convict, and imprison the criminal. The idea that much of law exists in order to replace and preempt the violent revenge that would occur in the absence of law, is a deep idea in our concept of law and we will return to it several times in this book.

A few years ago there was a brutal rape-murder of a fifteen-year-old girl. The police got a tip that the criminal was in a local bar, and they went there and were told by the bartender and some of the patrons that Mr. N, sitting in a corner nursing a drink, was the murderer-rapist. N was arrested, tried, and acquitted. The prosecuting attorney angrily complained to the press that the acquittal was a miscarriage of justice, brought about by the high-paid criminal defense attorney's use of dirty tricks. The family of the fifteen-year-old victim thereupon went after Mr. N, and killed him. Believing that the state had failed to do justice, they took justice into their own hands. The state then had no choice but to prosecute the family for murder.

The story is even worse than that. What actually happened at N's trial was that his attorney was able to prove that the bartender and other persons at the bar falsely accused N, because they knew who the real murderer-rapist was and were physically afraid of him. Thus it turned out that the prosecuting attorney's false and self-serving statement to the press that the trial was a miscarriage of justice was the real cause of the victim's family attacking and killing innocent Mr. N. The prosecutor made the statement because, as an elected official, he did not want the public to think he had prosecuted the wrong man. Thus, we see that the "social contract" theory of criminal imprisonment only works if the public perceives it to work; when the public is misled, as by the prosecutor in this case, then law can break down and people can take the law into their own hands.

4. Incarceration

A fourth theory of imprisonment for crimes is the incarceration theory. It's the simplest theory; it says that we put a criminal behind bars for the same reason that we cage a wild animal. The theory simply looks to the temporary protection of the public for the duration of the imprisonment.

5. Rehabilitation

Finally, there is the theory of rehabilitation. In the 1930s it was widely felt that with modern psychiatric counseling and improvement of prison conditions, criminals could be taught during their prison term how to fit in with society. However, in recent years, prisons have turned out to be institutions for learning how to commit greater and more violent crimes. Nevertheless rehabilitation is usually listed as a theory of criminal law.

Consider the possibility of a frontal lobotomy; the surgical removal of portions of the cerebral cortex can change a criminal's personality sufficiently to make any further criminal act extremely unlikely. Is such an invasion of a person's body worse than keeping the person behind bars for ten, twenty, or thirty years? If you think that it is more humane, you ought to consider further the ever-present possibility that an occasional convicted criminal is in fact innocent: for such a person, imprisonment at least carries the potential of an eventual reversal of the conviction without permanent personality change.[2]

Now, as to these five theories, which of them is dependent upon the premise of free will? Only the first, the theory of punishment. I contend that the other four are perfectly applicable even on the assumption that the criminal had no choice but to commit the crime. If you consider this issue and come to the conclusion that these other four are sufficient, in combination or even singly, to justify

[2] Does a convicted person have a right to be freed if he can show he was in fact innocent? For the most part, the law is unconcerned with actual innocence; it deems a person "guilty" who has been convicted at trial.

Once a person has been convicted and the conviction has been affirmed by the appellate court, his only further recourse to a court would be through the various procedures generally known as "habeas corpus." Habeas corpus is an ancient writ of law, going back to the Magna Carta. It says that a person who claims he is illegally imprisoned has a right to be brought before a court, and if the court finds that his imprisonment is in fact illegal, the court has the power to release him immediately. But can you see why innocence does not count as an "illegal" imprisonment? A person is lawfully in prison if a court of competent jurisdiction, and a jury of his peers, found him guilty of a crime. The fact that the jury may have made a mistake—and convicted an innocent man—is said by the law to be irrelevant. The law is only concerned with the fact that the jury found him guilty, not with whether he was in fact guilty. This rule works both ways. A guilty man may be mistakenly found to be innocent at trial. If so, he goes free, and the prosecutor can not try him again for the same crime.

The apparent injustice of the rule that an innocent man is lawfully incarcerated is currently leading the Supreme Court to rethink the basis for habeas corpus. The Court has held that the evidence presented at trial must at least suffice to convince a "rational trier of fact" that the defendant is guilty beyond a reasonable doubt. This is not the same thing as an innocence test, but it seems to be moving in that direction. At the same time that the Court is taking cautious steps to liberalize habeas corpus to allow at least a test of evidentiary sufficiency, it is also moving to disallow many of its earlier precedents regarding various assertions of illegality. Some trials have technically violated a defendant's constitutional rights, yet the overwhelming evidence at the trial was that the defendant was guilty. The Supreme Court is taking a hard look at precedents in this area, and moving toward a position that obviously guilty defendants will not be freed on a technicality, even if their constitutional rights were violated.

imprisonment, then you can agree with the organizing theory I've suggested: that the law generally does not depend on any assumption of free will.

More than that, you might want to reconsider the moral foundations of the theory of punishment itself. Since it has shown up as exceptional among our five theories, perhaps it is really out of place in a legal system. Maybe it builds upon subjective emotional factors that can result in injustice due to the difficulty of quantifying what we mean by proper and adequate punishment. Maybe the punishment never quite fits the crime. We will come back to this question of justice in Chapter 7.

D. DEGREES OF INTENTION

Let's move away from our focus on criminal law, and look at all kinds of law. Despite my emphasis on objectivity, the law does draw a distinction among different degrees of intention. It does so across the board, in criminal law, tort law, contract law, property law, and so forth. The intention spectrum runs, first, from acts that we clearly and rationally decide to do, second, to acts that we do recklessly, third, to negligent acts, and fourth to things that we did not intend at all.

Our organizing principle so far—that law is possible even if there is no assumption of free will—now helps us in determining these states of mind, these degrees of intentionality. For although much of the law concerns itself with states of mind, the evidence and proof of these states of mind are treated objectively by the law. The law does not attempt to "look into" a person's mind to see whether she voluntarily decided to act, but rather sets up certain standards that characterize states of mind irrespective of whether the person in question actually had that state of mind or not.

Here's an example of legal objectivity in a contracts case. Suppose I enter into a contract with an organization to give a lecture, and the organization agrees to pay me my average fee of $50,000.[3] But the contract omits anything about when the lecture is to be delivered. As soon as the contract is signed, the organization informs me that I must give the lecture in a week. I reply that I need to come up

[3] If they do, it will be the first time ever that they reach my average.

with a good idea for the lecture, and that might take a year. I add that the contract said nothing about when the lecture must be given, and the organization replies, "that's right, so it means that you have to give the lecture whenever we tell you to." I refuse, and the organization then sues me on the contract to get me to give the lecture right away. The contract is perfectly enforceable even though it says nothing about when the lecture is to be given. The judge, acting as factfinder, must interpret the contract as if it had a clause in it saying when the lecture is to be given. The judge stares at the blank space in the contract and proceeds to "read" what the blank says. The law tells the judge how to fill in the blank. The law says that the blank must be filled in with a "reasonable" time.

The "reasonable" time has nothing to do with my state of mind—what I thought the time should be—nor with the organization's collective thoughts on the matter. The organization says "one week" but since it is only one party to the contract, what it says cannot determine how the blank should be filled in. I say "one year," but for the same reason I cannot determine that the blank space should be interpreted to read "one year." Nor does the judge "split the difference" and say that the blank space is six months—the halfway point between the organization's position and my position. The "reasonable" time is none of these, even though the law invented the reasonable time standard as a substitute for what the parties intended. The intention of the parties may have given rise to the "reasonable time" interpretation centuries ago when it first came up in a contracts case, but since then the "reasonable time" standard has lived a life of its own. It has nothing to do with what the parties actually intended. The law in effect is saying, "we know what you intended even if you swear to us that you never intended it."

I don't know what the court would decide in this case. Much depends upon the judge, the quality of the arguments, the circumstances surrounding the making of the lecture contract, and for all we know, the weather on the day of the decision. The judge may say "three months." If so, that will be deemed the reasonable time. End of case.

In tort cases—cases where the plaintiff is harmed and is suing the defendant for money damages—the turning-point issue for the jury is often whether the defendant acted reasonably or prudently in the circumstances. The jury will not psychoanalyze the defendant but rather will decide whether a mythical reasonable person in the defendant's position would reasonably have acted the way the defendant acted. This is the way the law objectifies states of mind.

1. Intentional Acts

So let's begin with the first type of intentionality: acts that are clearly intended. For example, suppose a television evangelist embezzles funds from his ministry, and is subsequently brought up on criminal charges of embezzlement. Suppose his defense is: "God told me to do it. I had no free choice in the matter." Let's make the further assumption that the man is perfectly sincere and honest in saying this, and he is even able to convey to the jury his total sincerity. The judge, however, will instruct the jury that if the jury finds that the minister took funds which did not belong to him with the intent to convert those funds to his own use—that is, to spend the money on things for himself and keep what he bought—then they should find him guilty of the crime of embezzlement. The judge will tell the jury that it is irrelevant whether the defendant was acting under the strict orders of God. What matters is the objective fact that this defendant took these funds and intentionally converted them to his own use. Thus, even if the defendant has no free will at all, that fact is irrelevant if he took the money with the intention of converting it to his own use.

You might object, "but he cannot have taken the money *intentionally* if he was under the total influence of an outside Power, such as the Deity." That may be your definition of intentionally, but it is not the law's definition. The law says that intention is proven by the acts that the defendant did, and cares nothing about why. Intention is an objective, and not a subjective, fact.

There is a difference, however, if a defendant can prove that he had no idea what it was that he was doing. For if he can prove *that,* even the law will say that he could not have intended to do what he did. Thus, if the defendant was under hypnosis and believed that he was on another planet and the checks he was writing to himself drawn on the ministry's funds were really travel vouchers required by the extraterrestrial ministry of transportation—and of course it's not likely that a jury will believe all this—if a defendant can prove he had absolutely no idea of what really was going on, then the law would not hold him responsible.

Can you see how this case is distinguishable? In the previous case, the defendant knew that he was converting real money to his own use, but believed he was doing it under God's orders. But in the hypnosis case, the defendant presumably did not know that he was converting "money" to his own use. Even the average, reasonable person could be the victim of a hallucination, or under hypnotism, or whatever, and thus be totally controlled in his actions. In such a case, if you believe him, what he actually did was to sign extraterrestrial travel vouchers.[4] Thus, applying the law's objective test to his acts, we say that he did nothing wrong. Naturally, the more complicated the crime, and the more steps the defendant had to go through to commit it, the less we would believe any such defense.

Here is a further variation on our hypothetical case that I will leave as a problem for you to solve. The defendant argues that he was under hypnosis, and imagined himself to be on another planet working for an evil organization. Because he wanted to destroy that organization, he wrote checks on the organization's bank account that were payable to himself, and he cashed them. If you were the judge, would you find the defendant innocent or guilty of embezzlement? Why?

2. *Recklessness*

Let's take a different degree of intentionality—that which is called recklessness. A reckless act falls short of clear and deliberate intentionality. Suppose a pedestrian is hit by a car, and the driver of the car says, "I was so drunk that I had absolutely no control over the wheel; I didn't know what I was doing; I had no intention to run down a pedestrian." Now, we should put to one side the separate

[4] From an objective point of view, the human machine is defective when hallucinating, so that no matter what is inputted into the machine, the machine engages in "runaway" eccentric behavior that is stimulated, rather than deterred, by the inputs. In such a case, the machine cannot be controlled by varying the inputs; rather, one has to intervene in the machine directly (such as de-bugging it).

crime of drunken driving; as to that crime, the defendant driver of the car is clearly guilty. He may lose his license as a result. But the driver is facing a possible felony indictment. Is the driver guilty of criminal assault and battery in hitting the pedestrian?

The law will hold the defendant responsible for all those acts committed while he was drunk on the theory that he knew, before he got drunk, that driving under the influence of alcohol could result in injuries to other persons. The element of criminal intent, then, occurred when the defendant decided, at time t-0, to get drunk and then drive a car. What happened after he was drunk at time t-1 is then attributed to him, even though he may have been so drunk that he had no control over his actions including no specific intention to hit a pedestrian.

If we think of the drunk-driving case as one where the legally relevant decision was made at time t-0 and where its instrumentality carried out the actual act at time t-1, then the same legal result should follow even if two different people acted, one at t-0 and the other at t-1. That is why we are beginning to see some bartenders being prosecuted for selling too many drinks to persons they had reason to know would be driving a car after leaving the bar. The bartenders are acting at time t-0 by providing the drinks that led to the subsequent accident. We can even distinguish this case from the televangelist. If a drug was slipped into the televangelist's drink at t-0 that made him hallucinate that he was signing extraterrestrial travel vouchers instead of checks, then he himself committed no act at time t-0. Thus, whatever he may have been hallucinating at time t-1, he should not be held legally responsible for his acts at t-1.

3. Negligence

Our third category, negligence, comprises perhaps the bulk of accident cases. The objective theory of law predicts that the legal test for negligence will have nothing to do with the state of mind of the defendant who is accused of acting negligently. And indeed, the law says that a defendant is negligent if the cost to him of avoiding the accident that occurred—his cost of precaution—is less than the probability that such an accident would occur multiplied by the magnitude of the loss suffered by the victim of the accident. Thus, if a driver of a car knows his brake is defective but he fails to get it repaired, and then he drives his car, his brakes fail to hold, and he hits a pedestrian, he is guilty of negligence and must pay the victim's entire hospital bills and compensate the victim for pain and suffering. The formula is wholly objective; the fact-finder (judge or jury) has no need to inquire into the driver's actual state of mind.

4. Strict Liability

Consider now the fascinating cases called "strict liability" cases, which is our fourth category along the intentionality spectrum. Suppose the owner of a pit-bull dog has the animal fenced in, but a neighborhood teenager, on a "dare" from his friends, climbs over the fence, opens the gate, and the dog escapes through the gate, runs across the street and attacks a pedestrian. The injured pedestrian can of course sue the neighborhood teenager for damages, since the teenager was "negligent" under our previous test—the teenager could have made sure the accident would not occur at truly minimal cost—simply by not opening the gate. However, it could turn out that the teenager might not have any money and the pedestrian's hospital bills could be very high. Can the pedestrian sue the owner of the dog?

The attorney for the dog owner would argue that his client had absolutely no intention for the dog to be in a position to attack anyone off the owner's own premises. Indeed, the dog-owner took reasonable precautions; he erected a high fence to ensure that the dog would not get out. He had no reason whatsoever to foresee that a neighborhood kid would trespass onto his property and let the dog free. In short, not only is there no blameworthy state of mind that we can attribute to the owner, but he took every reasonable precaution and hence is not even negligent on an objective theory of negligence.

What result? The attorney for the dog owner is trying to convince the court to apply a negligence standard. Under that standard, the owner would not be held liable for the pedestrian's damages. But this argument won't work, because the court will not apply a negligence theory at all. The court will award the judgment to the pedestrian by holding the dog owner strictly liable.

Under the old case law, this was the "wild animal" theory, and strict liability—liability in total absence of intent—was found against the owners of lions, tigers, bears, elephants, wolves, some monkeys, and wild boars. Under the analysis I've been developing, we can look at the time t-0, which was the time when the owner made his initial decision to have a pit bull on his property. True, no one could have foretold at time t-0 exactly how the dog might ever be set free, or what the dog might do if freed by some unforeseeable agency. But remember at time t-0 the driver who decided to become intoxicated also could not know what accident might occur, if any, once he started driving the car. In the same way, we simply point out that the dog owner at t-0 decided to own a pit bull and put it in his front yard. That choice turned out to result in an accident to the pedestrian. The law holds him responsible, objectively, for the injuries caused by the dog because a pit bull dog is dangerous enough that anyone who takes the animal into a community is creating an abnormal danger to others. In such cases, the owner will be held liable for the animal's acts on a "strict liability" theory.

In all these cases, we see the law focussing upon the channeling of human behavior at t-0, the time when the presence of the law can make a difference in the behavioral decision reached by persons subject to the law. We don't need a subjective theory of free will to explain this; the law works simply by changing the environmental considerations inputted into the mind of the decision maker at time t-0, which is when the decision maker's mind is susceptible of being influenced. In other words, the law says that if you decide to own a pit bull or decide to get drunk, you're going to be stuck with responsibility for the consequences of those decisions. If you don't like those consequences, then you should not buy the pit bull or get drunk in the first place.

CHAPTER 2. WHAT LAW EMPOWERS US TO DO

The definition of the function of law that I set out at the beginning of Chapter 1 may have suggested to you that it is the government itself that consciously channels human behavior into socially desirable directions. Actually, the government is directly concerned with only a small part of the law. The government is of course concerned with the laws providing for taxation, for licensing, social security, foreign policy, immigration, public services such as highways, post offices, and national parks, but all of that adds up to just a fraction of the law. Most of the law regulates private conduct, the things that affect us in our daily lives. And much of this law originated in court decisions where one injured person sought redress against another person who allegedly caused the injury. The injuries I speak about could be injuries to the body, or financial injuries, injuries to reputation, or injuries to property. The way today's law affects us the most is in the provisions it makes for the rights and obligations that we have vis-à-vis other people.

A. TYPES OF LEGAL CAPACITIES

Let's take a look not at the substantive content of law, but rather at the forms and structures that law takes. Law doesn't just regulate us, it also empowers us. Consider the idea of a contract. From one standpoint, a contract is something a court can enforce, and by enforcing it the court constricts and regulates the actions of the parties. But from another, equally valid, standpoint, if it were not for the possibility of judicial enforcement of the contract, the contract as a mechanism would not exist. The possibility of enforcement, in other words, gives binding force to an agreement between two people, empowering those people to enter into a voluntary arrangement where each side knows that the other side will be legally bound to the terms of the contract.

Scholars have attempted to break down the bundle of legal capacities and empowerments into more primitive concepts. Let us consider what these concepts look like and do.

1. Rights and Duties

The idea of rights is the first and most obvious kind of legal capacity and empowerment that we might have. Does the idea of rights immediately suggest that there is a corresponding concept of duties? If I have a right, do you have a duty? For instance, if I have a right to freedom of speech, does that mean that you have a duty to listen?

You might concede that I have a right to speak, but you probably would not agree that you have a duty to listen to me. You would assert a privilege not to listen. Does that mean that I can have a right without anyone else having a duty or obligation? No, because my right to speak does not entail your duty to listen. We have to be a lot more precise. My right to speak only entails your correlative duty not to stop me from speaking. If I have a right to ride my bicycle, you have a correlative duty not to interfere with my riding my bicycle. If I have a right to the exclusive ownership of a piece of land, you have a correlative obligation not to trespass upon it.

2. Privileges

When I mentioned my right of free speech, I said that you have a "privilege" not to listen to me if you don't want to listen. My right to speak can make no demand upon you to listen. So now we have a third concept to add to rights and duties, namely, privileges. A privilege signifies your liberty from any right that someone else has. If we like, we can define "privilege" by using the language of duty. We can say: if you have a legal privilege with respect to X, it means that you have no duty regarding X.

3. Correlativity of Rights and Duties

I said that rights are correlative with duties, but as we have seen, we have to be clear about what duties we're talking about. The duty that is correlative with a right is not the duty to effectuate the right but simply a duty not to interfere with the right. The failure to understand this point has led many people to sneer at the idea of international human rights. Consider the Universal Declaration of Human Rights, adopted in the United Nations in 1948. Among other things it proclaims that everyone has the right to food, clothing, and housing; everyone has the right to work; everyone has a right to own property. But critics have viewed these human rights as empty propositions, on the ground that asserting someone's right to food does not mean that manna is going to fall from heaven or that the government is going to feed all its citizens. Putting the critical question more pointedly, we may ask: if a starving person has the right to food, does anyone have a duty to feed that person? Do we all have to stop everything we're doing and start feeding the starving people of this world? If our answer to this question is no, then the critics of human rights ask the next question: How can it make any sense to claim that a starving person has the right to food but to concede that no one has a legal duty to feed that person? And at this point, without even waiting for an answer, the critics conclude that there can be no such thing as a human right to food, clothing, shelter, or employment.

So let's test their conclusion against a concrete case. Suppose you send a CARE package of food to a starving Ethiopian family. You had no legal duty to send the package, but you decided to do it out of a moral sense of obligation. Suppose some Ethiopian officials attempt to confiscate that package when it arrives and sell it for their own personal gain. In fact, there have been widespread allegations that officials have done exactly that. If they did, would they be violating anyone's rights? Clearly they would be interfering with the right of the Ethiopian people to the food that was freely given to them. We can say that the human right of the Ethiopian people to food, recognized as a legal right under international law, creates a legal duty on the part of the government of Ethiopia not to interfere with the delivery of the CARE packages. In other words, the government of Ethiopia is under an international legal obligation to make sure that its own officials do not intercept the food.

We are not now talking about whether that legal duty will be enforced. But we can say that the legal duty exists, and that it *may* be enforced through diplomatic or foreign policy means. Thus, the existence of a human right to food makes a difference. Without it, the government officials of Ethiopia could take the food and sell it and pocket the proceeds and not be violating any law (we are assuming there is no Ethiopian law that would stop Ethiopian officials from doing this). But *with* an internationally recognized human right to food, the Ethiopian officials would be violating that right if they confiscated the CARE package. And someday in the future, perhaps, through an international court or some other mechanism, they could be found guilty and punished for transgressing this "right to food" of the Ethiopian people.

How about the right to work? We can look at the statement that everyone has a right to a job as a kind of aspirational ideal. It's one of the things we believe in on general moral principles. But we can also look on it as a legal statement that says: if someone wants to hire someone else to do a job, no third person has the right to interfere, and indeed, all other persons have a duty not to interfere.

The right-duty question has another dimension that takes us more deeply into the theory of a legal system. Suppose the neighborhood bully interferes with your bicycle riding. You say "I have a right to ride this bike; it's my bike." The bully may hear your words but shrug them off. If he is much bigger than you, he'll take the bike and ride away while you are ineffectually shouting after him, "But it's mine." Your assertions of right in this case have amounted to nothing but ineffectual rhetoric. The rhetoric has not stopped the bully from taking your bike away from you.

But you have a "friend" somewhere out there whom you can call in to help you. So you say, "if you don't give me back my bike, I'll call the police." Suddenly the long arm of the state has been invoked, and you and the bully are no longer in a purely bilateral situation. If the police come, they will consider the question of legal right and legal duty to be decisive. If you are indeed the legal owner of the bike, they'll forcibly take it away from the bully and hand it over to you. And this is what you counted on when you told the bully that you would call the police.

Thus, there appears to be something about rights and duties that requires us to go beyond a two-person bilateral situation and to look at the relationship trilaterally. Bilaterally, the "right" you asserted seemed to depend upon the bully's acceptance of it. But trilaterally this is not so, because the long arm of the state can intrude. Perhaps, upon analysis, the "right" you have is in fact a right to have the state enforce your claim against anyone else, such as the neighborhood bully. And maybe the duty that the bully has is another way of saying that the state will force him to behave in a certain way. Maybe, then, the notion of "legal right" means that you have a right against the state to enforce your claims against others. If they don't go along with your claims, the state will force them to. Under this view, which as we'll see later is highly "positivistic," rights and duties only exist where there is a state.

But on further analysis, do you or does anyone really have a "right" against the state? You can telephone the police, but do you have the right to force the police to enforce your right? If the bully is bigger than you, the state is bigger still, and it has all the guns. The state might turn a deaf ear to your pleas of right. So analytically aren't we back in the same box that we were in when we considered the bilateral situation?

If the state refuses to acknowledge your right, you can at least say that you have a claim against the state to enforce your rights. You can claim that the bully is violating your rights by snatching your bicycle, and you can call upon the state to enforce your claim of right to get the bicycle back.

Suppose the state refuses to respond to your claim. Suppose you make all the appropriate phone calls and write all the appropriate letters, but the net result is that the government says they don't feel like enforcing your asserted right. Is this analogous to the binary situation where you asserted a right against the bully which he denied? Not quite. When he took your bicycle, you still had a good claim of right against him, even though he denied it, because you had the potential of calling in the state to enforce your right. But now, when the state itself says that it will not enforce your right, there is no potential left. You may be forced to conclude that you don't have a legal right to the bicycle at all. Of course, this is very hard to imagine, because if the state denies that there is valid ownership of a bicycle, consistency would require the state to deny that anyone owns any personal property. And that would be a revolutionary claim that would upset a lot more people than bicycle owners.

So let me suggest a more plausible case. Suppose you and your friend agree to go to the annual prom. Because you're a little insecure about it, you ask your friend to sign a dating contract with you. The contract says that you will both show up at a certain place and time. Then in reliance on this agreement, you go out and rent expensive evening clothes, you tell all your friends about it, and so forth, but then on prom night your friend doesn't show up. You are heartbroken and you call the police, but the police laugh at you and thereby make you even more upset. So the next day you go to court and sue your friend for standing you up.

After due deliberation, the court issues the following opinion. The court finds that there is a valid legal contract for a date. It also holds that you reasonably relied upon the contract. It holds that your friend broke the contract, and that the breach of contract was unjustifiable. The court further finds that you suffered great mental and emotional stress, and you also lost money in renting evening clothes and purchasing two unused prom tickets. So far, so good. As you listen to the judge read the court's opinion, you think you have won. But then to your great surprise the court delivers its verdict. You lose.

We'll assume that the court gives no reason. You protest to the judge that her judgment is illogical, and she says, "sorry, it's just a matter of how I feel about it. Nothing personal; I just won't ever enforce a dating contract, no matter how many disappointed suitors might bring suit."

In this "trilateral" case involving you, the state, and the defendant, the situation is entirely different from the "bilateral" case involving just you and another person. In the bilateral case, as we have seen, you can make a claim of right against someone else, and that other person's rejection of your claim is not equivalent to defeating your right. But now in the trilateral situation, if the court rejects your claim, your claim is in fact defeated. (Of course you can appeal the decision to a higher court; but let's assume that all the appellate courts affirm the judge's initial decision.)

We are forced to conclude that you actually have no legal right to enforce a contract to go to the annual prom, or to the theater or ballet for that matter. Why? Perhaps there is no good legal reason for it; courts just do not enforce dating contracts. Maybe someday they will. When they do, a new right will be born. Until then, no matter what contract you sign, no matter how many witnesses, no matter how much money you spend in getting ready for the date, you just can't sue for breach of a dating contract. If the state says you don't have a legal right, then you really don't have one.

4. Entitlements

There is a better term for "legal rights." Most of the time when lawyers use the term "rights" they are thinking of legally enforceable rights where the state is involved in what I have called the trilateral situation. Legal scholars recently have been using the term "entitlements" when they refer to these legal rights. Although when we're talking about moral rights we can continue to use the term "rights," when we mean legally enforceable rights we should use the term "entitlements." If you have an entitlement to do something, you have a legal right to do it; that is, you have a claim against the state that you can reasonably expect the state to enforce.

Of course, not all rights are legal rights, and therefore not all rights are entitlements. You may have some fundamental moral rights that a particular country with its own particular legal system might not recognize as legal rights. Similarly there may be moral duties that are not legal duties. Here is an example of a clear moral duty. Suppose you're sunning yourself at the end of a pier, and you hear someone thrashing and splashing in the water below. There's a coil of rope next to you, one end of it tied to the pier. The stranger below yells up to you, "I'm drowning, throw me the rope." There is no doubt that a person in your situation has a moral duty to kick over the coil of rope to save the life of the drowning person. But is there a legal duty to kick down the rope? The answer depends upon what legal system you're in; in some countries yes, in others no. The United States is one of the countries which says no. In the United States, as far as the law is concerned, you can just sit there and enjoy the unique sight of someone drowning below you.

Because there is no legal duty in the United States to save the drowning stranger, it follows that the drowning person has no "entitlement" against you to get the rope. I should add that a few states in the United States are beginning to change this common-law result by the enactment of legislation.

Among other things, the case of the drowning stranger tells us that entitlements change depending upon what jurisdiction you're in; if you cross a state boundary or a national boundary, suddenly there is an alteration in the set of your entitlements. That's not true about moral rights and obligations; it's the very nature of moral duties that they remain the same even though you cross a political boundary. In Chapter 4 I'll say more about the relation between legal duties and moral duties. But for now let's concentrate on the legal side of the story.

5. Powers

We've looked so far at rights, entitlements, duties, and privileges, but these aren't the only basic relationships in the law. Another one that I mentioned briefly at the outset of this Chapter is that of "powers." Recall that the law empowers us to create legally binding relationships in certain areas, such as the power to enter into a contract, or make a will, or to deed your property over to someone else. Once you exercise that power, then a new bunch of legal duties crops up. For example, once you enter into a contract, then the law will enforce the terms of the contract. Once you make a will, then after your death—even though you won't know it is happening, unless you're Shirley MacLaine—the law will enforce the terms of that will through the probate court. It's interesting that the terms of your contract or your will become part of the law, they become legally enforceable, so you've invented some substantive law by your power to make a contract or a will. But in those few instances where the law you invent substantively conflicts with criminal laws, then you don't have a legal power to change the law. The criminal laws will override any private law you attempt to create through the exercise of a legal power. For example, if you make a contract with an assassin to murder someone, you pay the assassin money, and then the assassin cheats you and fails to go through with the killing, obviously the courts aren't going to enforce that contract for you. They won't even allow you to sue the hired killer to get your money back. Indeed, as soon as you file your complaint in court against the assassin, and provide a copy of the contract to back up your complaint, you are liable to be arrested then and there for attempted murder.

Any contract to commit a crime, not just the murder contract, is illegal and unenforceable. If I make a contract with you to pay you $5,000 if the Chicago Bears win the next Super Bowl, and you agree to paint the exterior of my house if any other team wins the next Super Bowl, we've entered into a "gambling contract" and the law regards it as void.

6. Immunities

Another capacity that the law provides is that of "immunity." We say someone has an immunity if he or she is exempt from the operation of a legal power. We're all familiar with a witness before a Congressional investigating committee who has been granted an immunity from prosecution. Why doesn't Congress simply pass a law making it a felony if a witness refuses to testify? In that way, Congress would not have to grant any witness an immunity from prosecution. The answer is that the United States Constitution does not empower Congress to enact such a law. The Fifth Amendment to the Constitution states that no person "shall be compelled in any criminal case to be a witness against himself." The Supreme Court has interpreted this clause as laying down a privilege against self-incrimination. So Congress cannot force a witness to testify if the result of that testimony is likely to form the basis for prosecuting that very witness.

The only way that Congress can compel testimony, therefore, is to cut out the possibility that the witness can be prosecuted for his or her testimony. So Congress may grant to the witness an immunity from prosecution. This immunity consists of a legally binding assurance that nothing the witness says will be used against him.

I said that the Supreme Court has interpreted the Fifth Amendment as constituting a *privilege* against self-incrimination. Since it is a privilege, any person may waive the privilege. Therefore we now have the full answer to the question why Congress gives immunity to the witness: it is a bargained exchange. The witness waives the privilege against self-incrimination, and receives in payment for that waiver a grant of immunity from prosecution. So a "privilege," like a "power," is something the law gives you but you don't need to exercise. You may waive a privilege and you may simply refrain from exercising a power.

B. TYPES OF ENTITLEMENTS

We begin to see some of the rich texture that the law provides to us. We don't simply have rights and duties; we also have entitlements, privileges, powers, and immunities. All of these together allow us to make at least a flat map of legal relationships. But it's still just a two-dimensional map. We want to go deeper into the types of rights or duties or privileges that we have. If we take the concept of "entitlements," we find that there are three different kinds of entitlements—property entitlements, liability entitlements, and inalienable entitlements. An entitlement not only has a location on our map, but it also has height and depth depending on the kind of entitlement it is. Let us consider the matter of entitlements, as it is a good illustration of the dimensional scope of law.

The differences among property, liability, and inalienable entitlements are best introduced by asking how we can *lose* entitlements that we have. We can lose a property entitlement by selling it or giving it away or simply destroying it. If I have an entitlement to my bicycle, I can give the bicycle to you and thereby lose my entitlement. But there is a class of entitlements the law gives us that we cannot sell or give away or even destroy: the inalienable entitlements. Those we're stuck with. Life and liberty are two of those inalienable entitlements, as the Declaration of Independence said. The law does not allow you to take your own life—suicide is against the law. The law does not allow you to sell yourself into permanent slavery, for liberty is an inalienable entitlement.

In between property and inalienable entitlements, as you might suspect, are liability entitlements. That represents a harder case. Before getting to it, let's consider some further examples of property entitlements and inalienable entitlements.

1. Property Entitlements

Tangible items that we own are examples of property entitlements; we own our pencils, books, and notepaper, and we can sell them, give them away, or toss them in the fire. Our own labor is an intangible item that we own. For example, lawyers own their own legal services; they can sell their services at so much per hour or donate them to a deserving client who cannot afford to pay. We own other intangibles, such as the money in our bank account, which of course is not really money in the bank but rather a promise by the bank to pay us in U.S. funds if we want to make a withdrawal.

2. Inalienable Entitlements

How about inalienable entitlements? You may own your own body, but you can't legally sell yourself into slavery. You own your body, but you can't legally destroy it by committing suicide. Of course, the law against suicide is hard to enforce,[1] but nevertheless there is a law against it. A fairly universal example of an inalienable entitlement is your right to vote: you can't sell it and you can't give it away. You can lose it if you are imprisoned for a felony. Another way of losing it is by dying—except in Chicago where somehow the entitlement is preserved after death by waving a magic wand.

Although an inalienable entitlement cannot be sold, there is a subcategory of inalienable entitlements that can be given away. You own both your kidneys and you can't sell one of them; however, you might be able to donate a kidney under suitable legal restrictions. Parents cannot sell their children, but they are able under suitable legal restrictions to give them up to an adoption agency. Many states are presently considering laws regulating surrogate motherhood, saying that a woman may not charge rent for her uterus but under suitable legal restrictions might be able to be a surrogate mother to accommodate a friend or a relative and bear the child so long as she doesn't charge the friend or relative for her services. Some states are

[1] I've always wanted to write a certain book just because I like the title I thought up for it: *Suicide for Beginners.* (It should be added to the one Steve Allen always wanted to write: *Brain Surgery Self-Taught.*)

considering allowing a uterus rental charge of up to but no more than $10,000 per pregnancy.

The sale of most form of sexual services, including prostitution, is also prohibited under the law of most states, and thus is another example of an inalienable entitlement. Similarly, the laws against paying college athletes for their services makes an inalienable entitlement out of the college athlete's physical talents. The law prohibiting child labor is another example.

Since inalienable entitlements come from the law, it follows that the law can change them. The fact that an entitlement is called "inalienable" today doesn't mean that the law can't "alienate" it tomorrow. For example, some libertarians have argued recently that a person ought to be able to contract himself into slavery if he chooses to do so. Their contention is that it is paternalistic for the state to prohibit a rational adult from doing anything he wants with his own life. Back in the seventeenth century, the philosopher John Locke—whose ideas had a powerful impact upon the founding fathers of the new American republic—wrote that enslavement is not contrary to natural law if it results from the victors in a war sparing the lives of the vanquished. If the victorious power would either slaughter the vanquished population, or enslave them, then Locke felt that enslavement was the "lesser evil." Libertarians today argue that if a situation arises where the only way the father of a family can obtain enough money to save his children would be to sell himself into permanent slavery, then why should the state make it illegal for him to do so? If the children perish from starvation as a result of the father's inability to sell himself into slavery, then wouldn't that be the "greater evil" in Locke's terms? Do you think the inalienable entitlement to liberty should be repealed?

3. Liability Entitlements

Now, what about the middle category—liability entitlements? It turns out that you can *lose* a liability entitlement through the operation of the legal system, but you are entitled to get back an objectively determined sum of money for what you've lost. For example, you may own some land that the state wants to use for a highway, and you may not be willing to sell the land to the state. The state then exercises its right of eminent domain, which means that it can take your land away from you, but only by paying you its market value as determined by a court. You therefore have a liability entitlement in your land.

A less obvious example is that of nuisances. Suppose a cement company wants to build a factory near your house on some vacant land that it has purchased. You and your neighbors might be so concerned about the amount of pollution that such a factory would generate that you might be able to convince the local zoning board not to allow construction of the factory. However, other citizens might welcome the idea of getting jobs in the factory, and their political force might be stronger than that of the local property owners. So the factory is built. Now, you once had an entitlement to breathe clean air, which you purchased when you bought your house—because we all know that houses purchased in a town free from heavy industry are more expensive. So you've paid for clean air, you have an entitlement to it, and yet the new factory is going to take it away from you. The law has given you a liability entitlement to the clean air. That means that the company can take the clean air away from you, but it has to pay you a sum of money to compensate you for the dirty air that they've replaced it with.

Suppose you say that no sum of money short of five million dollars will compensate you, because you want to remain living right where you're living and you don't want any pollution. If you had a *property* entitlement to clean air, then you could set a price of $5 million on it. You can even set a $5 million price tag on your bicycle; there's no law against it. Whatever property entitlements you have, you don't have to sell any of them, which is another way of saying that you can set any outrageous price you want on them.

But it's different with a liability entitlement. The cement company is going to get built, and you're going to get whatever price the court, and not you, sets on your loss of value due to the pollution. Suppose your house was evaluated, the year before the cement company announced its plans, at $80,000. As soon as those plans were announced, the market price of your house plummeted to $50,000, because the real estate market in your area would suddenly realize that a house near a cement plant is considerably less desirable than houses not near cement plants. A court would very likely award you the difference of $30,000 of the loss of value of your house. Thus the cement company would have to pay you $30,000. That's what your clean air entitlement is worth. But once you get the money, the cement company would have an entitlement to build its plant and go on polluting indefinitely. It will have paid for, and destroyed, your liability entitlement to clean air.

Our right to be free from injuries resulting from accidents is a liability entitlement. If you're the victim of an auto accident, a court will put a value on your injuries and assess the negligent driver of the car. Suppose you lose a leg in a severe accident; a court might award you, say, $200,000. That is of course a lot less than the value you would place on your leg. The court will not use the test of figuring what amount you would be willing to receive in order to part with your leg. (Can you see why?) You wouldn't *sell* your leg for a million dollars, but you can't sell your leg anyway since it is not a property entitlement—it's an inalienable entitlement. Yet, in the event of accident, your leg is protected only by a liability rule, which is why an objectively determined value of, in our case $200,000, is placed upon it.

We see from this last example that different types of entitlements can apply to the same item. For instance, an owner of land has a property entitlement to sell it or give it away, but the same land is only protected by a liability entitlement in the event the state wants to exercise its right of eminent domain. And if that owner is incompetent—for example, an insane person—then the land becomes an inalienable entitlement, meaning that the insane person cannot legally sell it or give it away and no one can buy it from that person during the period of insanity. (Eminent domain proceedings, however, would still be possible, since the insane person can be represented by a court-appointed attorney if necessary.)

C. ECONOMIC STATUS OF PROPERTY VS. LIABILITY ENTITLEMENTS

Why do we have liability entitlements at all? Why can't society get along with just property entitlements and inalienable entitlements? In the cement-factory case, couldn't the company just go around to all the people in the town and purchase their rights to clean air? If the people did not sell, then there would be no cement factory. This would be a sort of robust capitalistic system, the kind preferred by the philosopher Ayn Rand. Her books demonstrate an unvarying defiance of the state in all its ramifications, and since a "liability entitlement" is really a matter of the state coming in and taking something away from you without your consent (even though the state pays for it), Rand would have heartily disapproved of liability entitlements and instead championed property entitlements.

But even before we get to the question of whether a robust capitalistic system grounded entirely in consent would be preferable, we should ask whether it would be workable. Why shouldn't we simply require the factory's attorneys to go around from house to house and purchase from each resident, at whatever price each resident negotiates with the lawyers, a "right" of the factory to pollute the air?

The practical reason is that the transaction costs would be too high. Transaction costs, like "friction" in physics, are non-productive costs involved in getting the transaction accomplished, such as the costs of finding all property owners, contacting them, negotiating with them, paying for attorneys, and so forth. In addition to the high transaction costs, the company would also discover that some of the owners they contact will place an exorbitant value on their property. Indeed, as soon as it's known that the company is buying clean-air rights, everyone would be encouraged to be a holdout. Each landowner would think: let the company buy up everybody else's property entitlements, and then only I will be left. But if I don't sell, then all their other rights won't do them any good, because with my one piece of land I can block the construction of the cement factory. Since by the time they get to me they will have made an enormous investment in buying up everyone else's air rights, I can ask for ten million dollars for mine, or else no deal. This is my chance to make a real killing in real estate.

The fact is that nearly everyone will have these same thoughts. It would be next to impossible to get the factory built. No matter which town the factory attorneys go to, they will invariably run up against "holdouts." Yet doesn't the country as a whole need cement factories? Surely they must be located *somewhere.*

If every town says, "let some other town have the cement factory," there might be a national problem. But perhaps some towns might desire to have a cement factory. Let's look at the economics. A factory provides jobs and it pays taxes to the town. How much are these worth to the town? The increased tax revenues will benefit everybody in the town, while the new jobs will only benefit certain people in the town who want a new job. Moreover, there will be losses: the loss of clean air to the homeowners in the vicinity of the proposed factory. The homeowners who will lose that clean air are not the exact same people who want new jobs. So, some people stand to lose clean air and others stand to gain new jobs. If the town on the whole wants the cement factory badly enough, the town ought to figure out a way to compensate the people who stand to lose. It ought to figure out how to compensate homeowners for the degrading of their air.

So let's say the town's mayor talks with the cement company officials and asks them how much the company can afford to pay to purchase the right to pollute the air in the town up to a certain emission level which is consistent with the projected level of emissions of the prospective cement factory. The company replies that it would be willing to pay $1 million for these "air rights." We've already seen that any attempt by the company to purchase the air rights from the homeowners would run up against the "holdout" problem. But the mayor can offer to ask the town's zoning board to allow the factory to come into the town, in return for a payment of $1 million which will be distributed to the homeowners who will be affected by the factory's emissions. There will be no holdout problem, because the homeowners will not have any choice. Each will be given a share of the million dollars depending on wholly objective factors such as proximity to the cement plant and previous market value of the homeowner's property. (Naturally, the homeowners can challenge the town's actions in court, but courts will go along with the industrial-development plan of the town unless the homeowners can show that it was done in bad faith or that it bears no rational relationship to the amount of property loss due to the pollution.)

In other words, we've seen the workings of a liability entitlement scheme. The homeowners have a liability entitlement to clean air, not a property entitlement. Hence if it makes economic sense for the factory to move into your neighborhood, then like it or not the only compensation you will get for your loss of clean air is an objectively determined sum of money. You can't block the factory by being a holdout, because if you could—that is, if the law permitted property entitlements to clean air—no factories could ever be built because there will always be one or more holdouts. And this result is a general one; it does not apply just to factories. New theaters, football stadiums, ballparks, or museums invariably stir up local property owners who resist them for various reasons. If it weren't for liability rules, very few of these facilities would ever be built, and we wouldn't have cities as they are today. For interested readers, I further develop the economic analysis of this chapter in the appendix.

CHAPTER 3. WHAT IS LEGISLATION?

A. THE POSITIVIST DEFINITION OF LAW

The simplest definition of law that anyone has ever come up with can be found in the writings of the theorists of legal positivism. Positivism defines law as a command that is backed by a sanction, that is, a command that is enforced. In other words, the legislature passes a statute; the statute commands us to do something ("pay your taxes") or refrain from doing something ("don't rob banks"); and the entire military might of the state stands ready in the background to enforce that statutory command if we disobey it.

How do we know that is what the law is? The positivists answer: try disobeying the legislature, and you'll soon see what the law is. Thus, when the legislature commands you to pay your income taxes, if you don't pay your taxes the police will pay you a visit. And if you barricade yourself on your ranch and surround yourself with like-minded armed individuals who refuse to pay taxes, eventually the government will call out the army if necessary to enforce the law. Actually, the government rarely needs to resort to physical power. If you don't pay your taxes, the government simply attaches your bank account and garnishes your wages, and suddenly you find that you don't have any money. And so the government gets its tax revenue, with interest, without using anything more than a notice to the bank and to your employer. If you don't like what the government has done—for example, you say that income taxation is unconstitutional—then you have to bring a lawsuit against the government to get your money back. If you commence the legal action, the legal realists (whom we'll meet later) will point out that the first thing you will notice is that the judges in the court are themselves government employees who are dependent upon tax revenues for their salaries, and so they're not likely to be especially receptive to your idea that you want your money back.

So much for the "enforcement" part of the positivist definition. The more interesting part is the "command" part. When the legislature enacts a bill into law, it has issued—under the positivist theory we are discussing—a command. To whom is the command addressed? We've been assuming so far that the command is addressed to you and to me. The command can be either that we have to do something, such as pay our taxes, or refrain from doing something, such as robbing banks. In Chapter 2 we went through some of the forms that these commands can take, including the specification of rights and duties, privileges, powers, and immunities. The enactment of a power, for example, is a rather subtle form of command. It doesn't immediately command you or me to do anything. For example, the legislature passes a law regulating wills. If you want to make a will, you do it in a certain way, with two witnesses who are unrelated to the testator, and so forth. Where's the command in that? You don't have to make a will. But the command is there; it is in the form of a conditional statement. It says in effect, "if a person makes a will in the proper form, with the proper witnesses and so forth, and then that person dies, then various state officials are hereby commanded to carry out the provisions of that will by dividing the testator's estate in the manner provided for in the will."

So there is a command lurking there, even when the legislature enacts a power or a privilege or an immunity. But note, the command was addressed not to you or to me but to state officials. It told them what to do IF someone makes a valid will. So we might conclude that although some legislative commands are addressed to you and to me, such as the commands to pay taxes or not to rob banks, other commands are addressed to state officials, taking the conditional form of commands we have called "powers." State officials, in this latter case, only are commanded if you or I do something to trigger their response, such as executing a valid will or entering into a valid contract. Can we therefore conclude that some laws are addressed to you and me and some to officials of the state?

B. KELSEN'S OBJECTIVE VERSION OF POSITIVISM

The common sense answer would be yes, and it's probably the right answer. However, Hans Kelsen, a prominent twentieth century legal positivist, came up with an extraordinary idea that led him to answer that question in the negative. Kelsen said that there are no laws that are addressed to the public; rather, all laws are addressed solely to state officials. Moreover, all laws are conditional laws—not just the laws of wills and contracts, but all laws.

Let's test Kelsen's theory by looking at an actual law of the State of Illinois. According to the Illinois Revised Statutes, Chapter 18 (Criminal Law and Procedure), § 18-1:

> A person commits robbery when he takes property from the person or presence of another by the use of force or by threatening the imminent use of force.
>
> (b) Sentence.
>
> robbery is a Class 2 felony.

And we find in Chapter 38, § 1005-8-1 (a)(5), that a class 2 felony is one in which "the sentence shall be not less than three years and not more than seven years."

Does the language of this law, the chapters, sections, subsections, and so forth, sound as if it is addressed to you and me? The law defines what robbery is, and defines what penalty is attached to it. It seems to be part of a manual for the use of the police, prosecutors, judges, and prison officials. It seems to be addressed to state officials, and not to you or me. Kelsen would translate § 18-1 of the Illinois Statutes as follows: "*if* any person should commit robbery as herein defined, *then* the judges are hereby commanded to sentence that person to three to seven years, the marshal is hereby commanded to take that person to prison, and the warden is hereby commanded to lock that person up for three to seven years." According to Kelsen, the law against robbery is not addressed to you and me any more than the law specifying how to make a valid will or contract. All laws are simply commands to state officials. When a member of the public does something to "trigger" the "if" part of the conditional enactment, for instance by robbing a bank, the "then" part of the conditional enactment comes into play in the form of commands to state officials to take forcible action against that person.

If you thought in Chapter 1 that I went pretty far in claiming that law was objective and did not depend on free will or free choice, you now see in Kelsen an extreme objective theory of law. Law is so objective in Kelsen's theory that it isn't even addressed to the public. Kelsen would not even say that the red and green lights at the intersection are beamed into the brains of the drivers of the cars; rather, he would assert that the red and green lights are there simply to inform the traffic police which drivers they should arrest. The red light is simply a signal to the traffic cop to issue a ticket to any driver who fails to stop at the red light. In Kelsen's view, if the driver of a car is alert enough to notice that traffic cops give tickets to drivers who go through red lights, then the alert driver can prevent this assertion of the wrath of the state by stopping at the red signal.

Under Kelsen's philosophy, we will stay out of jail only if we become aware of the patterns of behavior of the police and other state officials. One way of becoming aware of their consistent patterns of behavior is to look up the commands that they themselves follow. These commands are what we call "statutes." They consist of directives to police and other officials. By noticing what these commands tell the police to do, we can avoid getting into trouble. If a command tells the police to arrest robbers, then we can avoid getting arrested by the police if we refrain from committing robbery. The law, under Kelsen's extreme objectivism, doesn't tell *us* to do anything. We are simply the victims of an impersonal legal regime.

We could even improve a bit on Kelsen; we can dispense with the traffic cop. Instead, we mount a machine gun above the intersection, and if any car goes through the red light, a photoelectric cell is activated which is connected to the machine gun. The machine gun then shoots several rounds of steel-penetrating bullets through the roof of the offending vehicle. Now we finally have a purely objective, purely mechanical legal system. Undoubtedly many drivers will learn to stop on the red signal, and those who don't will be eliminated from the system entirely. In Darwinian terms, the nonconformists will be selected out, and we will be left with law-abiding individuals.

There's a real-world example that comes fairly close to the mounted machine gun. Have you seen those curved spikes set in the entrance to some parking lots, where you drive your car over the spikes and nothing happens, but if you try to go in the opposite direction—for example, you've parked and now don't want to pay at the exit gate so you try to back out through the entrance—the spikes will puncture all your tires? We have here an example of a purely self-enforcing mechanistic system. If suddenly a fire breaks out ahead of you in the parking lot, and you want to back out of there in a hurry, try arguing with those curved spikes.

It would be a mistake to dismiss Kelsen so readily as my rather sarcastic example of the machine gun seems to suggest. His purely objective theory of law is useful in bringing out certain salient features of the legal system and provides a heuristic model for us to question certain of those features.

Most importantly, Kelsen's theory implies that there is no necessary requirement of communication between the legislature and the public in a legal system. Let's consider the traffic signal again as a simple kind of law. Although it looks as if it's a command addressed to drivers, Kelsen says it's a communication from the legislature to the police. In fact, it doesn't even have to be a communication; it can be a kind of program that is itself inaccessible to the public. The legislature simply programs the state computer, and the state computer—which consists of police robots, judicial robots, prison robots, and so forth—simply processes that program. To be sure, in the case of the traffic signal, the public is given a good clue as to what is going on. The public figures out that by stopping on the red and going on the green, the various state officials will not be galvanized into repressive action. And so, a driver stops on the red light and avoids incurring the sanction of the traffic officer. This is a learned response on the part of drivers to state police behavior. Kelsen's approach is not unlike Pavlov's dogs who probably thought that by salivating at the sound of a bell they were signalling Dr. Pavlov to bring in some food.

If we look at some of the complex, convoluted legislation passed by Congress, it might as well be a set of computer commands in FORTRAN or PASCAL. How is any member of the public supposed to understand the complexities of the Internal Revenue Code? The Code, in some of its sections, is so complex that most Internal Revenue agents cannot understand it. Eventually someone in the government understands it, and then penalizes the taxpayer for failure to comply with the provisions.

But let us extend the complexity argument a bit. Laws that are apparently simple to understand often turn out to be construed by the courts in a strange way. We read in the daily papers of "surprising" decisions in cases, where most people thought the law said one thing but the judge said it meant the opposite. What is a member of the public to do in order to adjust his or her life in such a way as to stay out of jail?

Kelsen's answer is simple: hire a lawyer. A lawyer, to Kelsen, is a person who *translates* for clients the commands that Congress issues to the police. Your lawyer tells you what taxes you have to pay on certain kinds of income. Your lawyer tells you, for instance, that the "right turn after stopping on red signal" rule now being adopted by most states can also mean, in your state, that you can make a left turn after stopping on a red signal provided that you are on a one-way street and the street you are turning into is a one-way street. The statute itself may not say exactly that. The statute might be drafted in terms of allowable turns when not crossing an intersection. But that, as far as the public is concerned, is only computer talk between the legislature and the police. It is the attorney who translates that talk so that the public can understand it. For these translation services, the public pays considerable amounts of money to attorneys. The more complicated the rules become, the more money attorneys make. Is it any wonder that the complicated rules are usually *drafted* by attorneys on congressional staffs?

Law, then, is in Kelsen's view a kind of commodity in information. Lawyers manage to get hold of statutes and other sources of law, read them, translate them, and sell the translations to the public. The public will purchase the information from the lawyers because the public wants to know what it should do to stay out of trouble from state officials.

Let us consider a simple example of this translation process. Suppose a waiter asks a lawyer whether he must report his tips on his income tax forms. The lawyer pulls down from her shelf her massive copy of the Income Tax Code of 1954 as amended. The lawyer reads various sections in the Code that are messages from Congress to the Internal Revenue Service. These messages are written by lawyers in such a way that only lawyers can understand them. The lawyer finds that if an employee fails to report tips each month to his employer, then penalties will be inflicted. There is no penalty if the total amount of tips for the month is less than $20. Otherwise, penalties include an additional 50% of the tax on the tip income, plus $50 penalty for each month that the employee failed to report the tips. Having read all this, the lawyer informs the waiter that tips are reported not to the I.R.S. but to one's own employer. If the waiter fails to report the tips he received to his employer each month, he can expect to incur those penalties unless he received less than $20 a month. Once the penalties are assessed, the I.R.S. can collect them from the waiter's future wages, from his bank account, or they can force the sale of his personal assets and collect the penalties out of the proceeds of sale. And that's it; that's all the law is. The lawyer doesn't tell the waiter, under Kelsen's theory, to report the tips to his employer; all she tells the waiter is what state officials are likely to do if the waiter doesn't report the tips. This example should raise a number of questions in your mind about the law. Let us consider some of the implications.

1. Ignorance of the Law

What does Kelsen's theory do with the well-known saying about law that the public sometimes finds hard to understand: that "ignorance of the law is no excuse." When you first encountered that phrase, you may have said to yourself, "How unfair! How unjust! I'm supposed to obey certain laws even though I don't even know that they exist." Consider our waiter. I assumed that he knew enough to ask a lawyer the question whether he should report his tips as income. But a lot of people who take a job waiting on tables don't know enough to ask this question. They simply assume that a tip is a gift, a gratuity, something that the customer may give as a kind of thank-you for services that the customer was entitled to receive even in the absence of a tip. These waiters are then surprised when someone tells them, "No, any tips you receive are just like salary, and they have to be reported to the employer."

Let us analyze this situation the way mathematicians work out indirect proofs. We begin with the assumption that we want to disprove, and then show that it ends up in an impossibility or a contradiction.

So, we assume that ignorance of the law *is* an excuse. On that assumption, we can be sure that waiters would be encouraged never to find out about the income tax treatment of tips. There would be a sort of tacit practice in the waiting profession never to mention the subject, and if an old experienced waiter knows that tips are income he's supposed to keep it to himself and never inform the young waiters. As long as the young ones are never informed, then they can get away without reporting their tip income because they can always say that they were ignorant of the law.

We immediately see that this would put a great premium upon ignorance. Widespread ignorance of the law would become highly desirable. People would avoid asking lawyers for advice, and the income of the legal profession would nosedive—something lawyers certainly would be against. And then Congress would have to run all kinds of commercials on television, informing people about the law. A commercial might show, for example, a waiter pocketing a tip and then a booming voiceover saying "you must report all tips to your employer every month." And then people would retaliate by ceasing to watch television and we might all be better off—except for the general anarchy that would set in because there would be widespread noncompliance with the law. Since no one, least of all the government, wants anarchy, it is unlikely that any legal system in any nation at any time in history would consider ignorance of the law to be an excuse. Hence we've disproven our original assumption, and in fact proven the converse: that ignorance of the law can never legally be an excuse to disobey the law, because that would destroy the legal system itself.

What would Kelsen say about ignorance of the law? Clearly he does not need the formal proof we've just gone through. Under his theory, not only is ignorance not an excuse; it is entirely irrelevant. People only learn what the law is when they discover what actions officials take. And if they fail to learn, they wind up in jail. Kelsen would not even inquire whether people knew what the law was, since the law is not addressed to the people at all.

2. Secret Laws

Kelsen's explanation has the virtue of simplicity. By arguing that the law isn't addressed to the public in the first place, Kelsen's theory of law is complete at that moment in time when the legislature tells public officials what to do.

Here's a mental experiment we can make that would test the application of Kelsen's theory. Suppose someday the legislature in your home state decides to turn off all the traffic signals to save money, leaving it to the drivers to guess when to stop and when to go. However, traffic officers at the intersections are beeped on their radios when the lights would have been green and when they would have been red. Then they simply arrest all drivers who guess incorrectly. Should we call this strange and unfair system of traffic regulation "law"? Kelsen would.

A similar example, more outrageous and unfortunately true, concerns the "secret" laws in Nazi Germany, laws that were communicated only to the Gestapo. The Gestapo could arrest people for violating a secret law, a law that the people they arrested had no possible way of knowing. You could commit a crime in Nazi Germany without having any way of knowing that what you were doing was a crime. Of course it gave virtually unlimited power to the Gestapo. Were those "secret laws" deserving of the term "law"?

My use of this example against Hans Kelsen, who was a refugee from Nazi Germany, might be very unfair. Yet his theory, if taken to its extreme, says that secret laws are laws.

Secret laws violate our innate sense of justice. Yet they point out the fact that under positivism a legislative command is a complete law. Positivism has nothing to do with justice. Kelsen insists on a clear intellectual separation of the concept of law from that of justice; the justification of law, according to him, lies not in the law itself but in religion or social metaphysics. Kelsen's philosophy simply underscores the irrelevance of justice to the positivist view of law. A legislature can pass an unjust law; to the positivist, working under the "command" theory of law, an unjust law is still "law." Hence, if positivism admits laws that are substantively unjust, even outrageously unjust (for example, a law removing all political and legal rights of a minority group), then it would seem that a "secret" law is simply another variety of injustice.

3. Impossible Laws

If you are not happy with the laws of your state, then, according to Jeremy Bentham—the great positivist of the early 19th century-what you should do is change the legislature. Bentham felt that since the legislature reacts to popular will, a legislature that enacts outrageous laws is doing what the people want. Bentham would have had no problem with the law Woody Allen proclaimed as soon as he became dictator of the island of Marcos in the movie *Bananas*: from now on, he proclaimed, everyone will speak Swedish. Bentham would go even further. Imagine a legislature commanding that each person must, once a day in the town square, jump unassisted twenty feet into the air. Since the law is physically impossible to comply with, everyone in that town would be guilty of violating it. At least under Woody Allen the people could learn Swedish; but under Bentham, the law is valid even if people cannot possibly comply with it.

Suppose you're in the town square and a police officer comes up to you and says, "well, aren't you going to jump twenty feet high?" You say you cannot do it. The police officer then arrests you for violating the law. You are outraged, but outrageousness does not count as a legal excuse. You say that no one can comply with the law and the police officer answers, "you're right—that's why I can arrest anybody I want."

The positivists, especially including Kelsen, maintain that the twenty-foot command is "law." Does that suggest that positivism may not be a wholly satisfactory account of what "law" is? We will be coming back to this question in succeeding chapters.

4. Retroactive Laws

Can you imagine anything worse than a secret law or an impossible law? Competing with these for top spot on the list of the all-time worst laws are retroactive laws. Imagine a law that is passed today that makes it a crime for having done something that you did yesterday. Suppose if I were dictator, I made it a crime if anyone drank orange juice yesterday. Not only would you not have had any notice of the "crime," but you could not have even guessed at its possible content and avoided it; at least with my traffic signal case, where the signals are shut off and only the police know what they are, you could make a guess, or you could refrain from driving a car at all. You might even guess the secret laws of the Gestapo if you observed their pattern of arrests over a period of time. But a retroactive law is a total surprise because it nails you for something you already did. A retroactive law goes beyond and even contradicts the objective theory of law that I talked about in Chapter 1, because the objective theory presupposes that the legal message will make a difference at some point, we called it t-0, in human behavior. But a retroactive law cannot possibly shape or channel human behavior, because the behavior has already occurred at the moment in time when the law is created.

Nevertheless, positivism says that if a legislature enacts a secret law, an impossible law, or a retroactive law, they are valid laws. There is nothing to stop the legislature from enacting any law it wants, no matter how absurd its content or unfair its enforcement. In my orange juice case, you'd know the law was a valid law when the police throw you into jail.

You might wonder what the Constitution has to say about all of this. In the United States, secret laws or impossible laws would violate the Due Process clause of our Constitution; so would most retroactive laws, although there have been some minor instances of retroactive laws, for example tax laws, that have been upheld by the courts as constitutional. But all that is just an account of the present content of the United States Constitution. Theoretically, a constitution might provide anything. A constitution, which under positivist theory is simply a set of higher commands, could explicitly provide that the legislature may enact retroactive, secret, or impossible laws. If it did, then such laws would be valid under that constitution. So, the presence of a constitution does not affect the theory of positivism we're talking about; rather, it just sets the problem back one step, back from the legislature itself to the constitution under which the legislature is empowered to enact laws. Strictly speaking, under positivist theory the analysis remains unchanged if there is a constitution in the legal system.

Recall the definition of the function of law at the beginning of Chapter 1. How can a retroactive law possibly function to control people's behavior? Perhaps this is another clue that positivism may not be a complete account of what "law" is. In Chapter 4, we will consider whether there is an alternative to positivism. If there is, we will have to go back and reconsider the initial positivist definition of law as a command backed by sanction. We will see what an alternative theory would say about secret laws, impossible laws, or retroactive laws.

C. ALLOCATION OF LEGAL POWER BETWEEN LEGISLATURE AND COURT

But for the present, staying entirely within positivist theory, a major problem for the positivist remains to be reckoned with. The problem is that it is all well and good for the legislature to issue commands, but how are the commands to be applied? Commands are not self-executing; they require some sort of machinery to monitor the conduct of individuals and determine whether that conduct is in conformity to the commands. Without such law-applying machinery, the commands are likely to be ignored. Therefore positivism needs a mechanism to determine whether or not people are complying with the law, and to penalize those people who don't comply.

And so, courts come into the picture. The courts are the machinery charged with making sure that the law is applied correctly. And suddenly the picture emerges of a very useful, efficient, and functional partnership between the legislature and the court. The legislature makes general commands; the court applies these general commands to particular instances of conduct. The legislature then doesn't have to worry about the millions of cases of interpretation and application that will come up under any given law it enacts; it can leave that job of particularistic application to the court. And the court, in turn, doesn't have to worry about the content of the law or whether the law is the right law for the society; it simply applies whatever law the legislature enacts.

There is another difference that we can add to the one just mentioned (legislatures pass laws of general application, courts apply them to specific instances). It is that legislatures, for the most part, look forward while courts look backward. The legislature can enact any law it wants, but most laws that it enacts will take effect from the moment of their enactment and extend their effect into the indefinite future, until some later legislature changes the law or abolishes it. The legislature is not bound by any previous laws, because the legislature at any time can change or abolish previous laws. So the legislature, contemplating the future and deciding to alter it, enacts laws that have prospective effect only.

I've been qualifying my statements by saying "for the most part," because as we have seen, it is possible for the legislature to enact a retroactive law. But usually legislatures don't do this, and many countries have constitutions prohibiting it. Even if a country has no constitution, however, the legislature is unlikely to pass retroactive legislation. Such legislation is invariably perceived by the public as being grossly unfair, and it may lead the public to revolution or at least to voting out of office those legislators who supported the retroactive legislation. More than that we can see a systemic reason why legislatures tend to stay away from retroactive legislation. They find that a considerable source of their power to enact whatever laws they desire comes from a general public perception that it's all right for the legislature to change a law provided that everyone has notice of the change and can change their conduct accordingly. Take for instance the traffic rule allowing a right turn on red signal, which Woody Allen described as California's sole contribution to our culture. If Illinois, which presently has that rule, wants to abolish it, people won't be overly upset as long as the legislature gives everyone notice that the rule will be changed as of a certain date. People would get very upset, however, if the legislature changed the rule retroactively or secretly. Thus, a large part of the legislature's political power to enact whatever laws it desires to enact exists because the legislature does not attempt, or at least does not attempt very often, to change the law retroactively or secretly. Indeed, it is so commonplace for legislatures to change the law from the present to the future that we normally think of legislation as having only prospective effect.

In contrast to the legislature, the court—like the famed dodo bird—only looks backward. It applies the law retroactively to situations that have already occurred. The litigating parties before the court have already done whatever they've done, and now they are disagreeing as to the legal implications of what they've done.

Some readers will know that there are a few exceptions to the dodo-bird principle. Courts may act prospectively in those infrequent cases when it issues an injunction or makes a declaratory judgment, but even then, the injunction and declaratory judgment are based primarily on established facts and not speculative future facts. But let's put aside injunctions and declaratory judgments just as we put aside retroactive legislation, and say that for the present purpose courts are in the business of applying law to facts that have already occurred. They are supposed to look backwards, not forwards. Once somebody has already acted, the courts tell him whether what he did was legal or illegal.

Thus, the legislature legislates for the future, and the judiciary adjudicates for the past. Which has more power? At first blush, it might appear that the legislature has more power; after all, they are dealing with what's going to happen and therefore they can make a difference as to what people do, whereas the courts are dealing with what has already happened and which cannot be changed. More than that, the legislature can do whatever it wants with respect to the future; it can enact any law it wants to enact, as if writing on a clean slate. The court, on the other hand, has no power to change the law; the slate is full when the court looks at it. The court must simply apply existing law to the past facts in each case.

So, if you had to pick, which institution would you say has more power—the legislature or the court? Bishop Hoadley said, "Nay whoever hath an absolute authority to interpret any written or spoken laws it is he who is the lawgiver to all intents and purposes and not the person who first wrote or spake them." Maybe the good bishop was thinking of the laws of the church, but what he said applies to the laws of the state. The legislature might enact whatever statutes it cares to enact, but the courts can say what the statutes mean.

Suddenly we see that the courts, in principle, have unlimited power. Bishop Hoadley used the phrase "absolute authority." If courts can interpret without limit what a statute means, then the power of the legislature can be reduced to zero. The courts could say that statute X means Y, and the legislature would be powerless to prevent that radical reinterpretation because *whatever* the legislature might say—including statutes that remove from office all those judges who said that X means Y—would also have to be interpreted by the courts. If courts have the power to say that any legislation means whatever the courts want it to mean, and if courts exercised that power without limit, courts would have absolute power over the law and legislatures would have no power at all.

You can make a very practical objection here. You can say that courts do not typically act in such a way as to thwart the legislature. There is hardly any evidence of willful judicial behavior that radically reinterprets statutes, changing their plain meaning. So maybe there is no practical problem. Courts simply interpret statutes in good faith. They simply ascertain the legislative intent and go ahead and interpret the statute according to that intent. Hence, the positivist theory is saved; legislatures do issue commands, and courts effectuate those commands in good faith.

Is that the end of the story? Can we be sure that courts effectuate the legislative meaning? We can be fairly sure that courts act in good faith. What we now have to investigate is whether a court, acting in good faith, can possibly figure out what the legislature intended its statutes to mean. And *that* is a very practical problem indeed, because it goes to the heart of what the practicing lawyer does for a living—the interpretation of statutes and the practice of convincing courts as to the meaning of statutes.

Consider the Illinois statute I quoted earlier about robbery: "A person commits robbery when he takes property from the person or presence of another by the use of force or by threatening the imminent use of force." Let's just take one of the many possible ambiguities in this statute: the word "property." Here's a case where the word "property" becomes ambiguous.

Suppose someone steals my bicycle, and the next day I see that person riding the bike and I threaten to hit him with a stick. He jumps off the bike and I take it and start to ride away when a police officer arrests me. I am taken before a magistrate, and I say that it was my own bicycle. But the magistrate looks at the statute and says that the word "property" is unqualified. The statute doesn't say that the property has to belong to the victim of the robbery; it doesn't say anything about ownership of the property. The magistrate then rules that I have committed a three-to-seven year felony in robbing my own bicycle.

Why can't the court, or in my case the magistrate, go back to the legislature and ask whether they meant to include as robbery a case where the robber robs back his own property? Let's look closely at this question. Would the legislature be the same legislature that enacted the robbery statute? Suppose Illinois enacted the statute three years before the incident with my bicycle; if the magistrate now asks the legislature, there will be legislators there who were not present three years ago, so the legislature itself wouldn't be the same. But, then, what if the legislature had just enacted the robbery statute one week before the bicycle incident? Let's look at some of the difficulties.

One legislator might say, "of course I didn't mean that the statute I voted for should apply when someone takes back his own property." But another legislator says, "I've seen the newspaper reports of this bicycle case, and let me say here and now, I am in favor of law and order, and I don't want any criminal to take advantage of any loophole, so I voted for the statute with the idea in mind that it would cover every conceivable case of robbery regardless of who owned the property, even if the robber himself owned the property." Can we really be sure that both legislators are telling us exactly what was on their minds when they voted for the statute?

Here's another complication. What if the majority in one house of the Illinois legislature thought that "property" included the robber's own property but the majority in the other house thought it didn't include the robber's own property? How do we then decide what the legislature as a whole meant? And what about the governor, who could have vetoed the legislation? Should the governor's thoughts on what the statute meant be more important than the legislature's?

A third problem is whether legislators might respond to the magistrate's question by saying how they would interpret the statute now, rather than accurately reporting what they meant when they passed it. Sometimes a person cannot honestly remember whether a particular thought came to mind in the past, but probably most legislators would have clear positions about the robbery statute once the case came up and became a matter of public and political interest.

Suppose then that instead of the court asking the legislators what they had in mind when they enacted the robbery statute, the court asks the legislators right now to define, in the present, what the word "property" means, by passing a new bill defining that word. Now recall that our initial premise is that the court wants to know what the word "property" means because of my bicycle case. So I can expect my attorney to object to the idea of the legislature passing a new law in the present to define what the word "property" in the statute means as applied to my own case. My attorney might say, "Wait a minute, the alleged crime has already occurred, and you can't ask the legislature now to define the crime. Either it was robbery or it wasn't robbery at the time D'Amato snatched his bicycle back, but we can't determine what it was in the past by asking the legislature in the present to pass a definitional statute. Indeed, there's a term for what the court is proposing. It is a 'bill of attainder.' Any present legislative determination of the criminality of conduct that has already occurred is a bill of attainder, prohibited by the U.S. Constitution."

My attorney's argument should be persuasive in the United States. The U.S. Constitution does prohibit bills of attainder, which are a form of retroactive legislation. But we should leave the constitution out of it, since positivist theory can't depend for its validity upon whether any particular country has a particular constitution. Yet my attorney's argument ought to be persuasive in any country regardless of the constitution, because she is claiming that what the legislature says in the present might unfairly change what it meant in the past, and this would be the sort of injustice that should deter a court from applying to the legislature for a definitional statute.

In short, since the legislature deals prospectively, it cannot normally define crimes retroactively. On the other hand, the court only deals retroactively; it only deals with facts which have already occurred. So we conclude that the court cannot ask the legislature for guidance on what the word "property" means in the Illinois robbery statute, or ask any legislature anywhere what any of its words means.

This could strike you as a rather surprising result. Recall that we have posited a situation where the court desires to interpret the statute the way the legislature wanted it to be interpreted. But we now see that there are insuperable barriers to ascertaining how the legislature wanted the robbery statute to be interpreted. And these barriers always apply to every case. No court can "know" or even find out what the legislature truly intended a statute to mean.

What the court typically does is ask the attorneys in the case to argue about what the legislature must have intended. And this often calls for considerable imagination on the part of the attorneys. In my bicycle case, the magistrate might ask the attorneys why the legislature failed to qualify the word "property" in the robbery statute. The prosecutor speaks first. He argues that the legislature's failure to specify who owned the property when it could easily have done so indicates that the legislature intended to cover even the case where a person steals his own property.

My lawyer now will have to come up with a plausible reason why the legislature did not specify who owned the property. My lawyer could of course look at the debates in the Illinois legislature to see if the legislature might have alluded to this problem, but she will probably discover that, as in most ordinary criminal statutes, the legislative history is thin or nonexistent. So she will have to resort to creativity. She might say something like this: if the legislature had specified that the property had to belong to the victim of the robbery, then what would happen if A robbed B, a bank, and upon being arrested A claimed that the money he took was not the bank's own property at all, but belonged to C, the customers of the bank? Then A would claim that the robbery statute did not apply, because the statute specified that the property had to belong to B, the victim, in order for there to be robbery. So, my attorney argues, maybe the legislature deliberately chose to avoid this kind of complication; maybe it did not want the prosecutor to have to discover whose specific property it was in order to indict A for robbery; and maybe that's why the legislature didn't identify the ownership of the property in the robbery statute. But, she concludes, it is highly unlikely that any legislator ever thought of the possibility that a person might be indicted for stealing back his own property. The statute failed to qualify the word "property" because the legislature was only thinking about the complications that would be involved in every robbery indictment if the prosecutor had to prove whose property it belonged to; but the legislature never intended to suspend the ordinary meaning of words, which as everybody knows, rules out robbery if the robber robs his own property. In sum, my attorney argues, since there is a perfectly adequate reason for the legislature's having failed to specify whose property it was—the bank robbery hypothetical case—that answers the court's question without forcing the court to construe the statute to apply to the case where the robber steals back his own property.

Note that we have had to rely upon the imagination of attorneys and arguments in a courtroom about what, objectively, the legislature might have intended, while disallowing any attempt by the court to go back and ask the legislature what it actually had in mind. And in this sense, Bishop Hoadley is right in saying that the courts have "absolute authority" to interpret the laws.

But this conclusion is very troubling for positivists. How do they deal with it? How do they reestablish legislative supremacy in a system where the courts have the ultimate authority to interpret statutes enacted by the legislature? If "law" is a command by the legislature, we've now seen that the "command" can be changed or thwarted by the interpreter—even if the interpreter acts as fairly and rationally as possible to ascertain what the legislature might have meant.

1. Bentham's Solution

We start with the father of positivism, Jeremy Bentham, a tireless advocate of law reform in England at the beginning of the nineteenth century. Bentham's writings are so voluminous that they haven't yet been entirely collected and published. Bentham must have seen the courts in England in much the same light as Dickens did in the novel *Bleak House.* Dickens had described a probate court case involving the supervision and distribution of the assets of the Jarndyce estate. The case had dragged on over one hundred years. New beneficiaries were born, grew up, and died, and still the distribution of the assets was not resolved. Indeed, with each new potential beneficiary that was born, the case itself was rejuvenated because all the pleadings had to be changed to take into account the new heir. As Dickens observed, the day the case would finally come to an end would be the day when all the money in the estate would be used up in paying lawyers' fees and court costs.

Bentham believed, with good reason at his historical time, that the courts were playthings of the rich, and that the only way to bring justice to all the people was through Parliament, because Parliament at least responded to the power of the vote. Bentham realized that courts were needed to apply the law that Parliament enacted. So what he tried to do was to systematically cut away the discretion the courts enjoyed by making legislation more and more comprehensive.

In particular, Bentham advocated the enactment of civil codes, and his pleas for codification enjoyed enormous success around the world. In Latin America, in particular, most countries have civil codes that owe their origins to the advocacy of Jeremy Bentham. For Bentham, a civil code was a clear, comprehensive, and dense statement of all the law. A citizen could just look up the law in the statute books, and not have to speculate upon what a court might decide. The more particularistic and dense the legislation, the less room there would be for judicial creativity and judicial discretion.

But no matter how brave, bold, and fresh Bentham's views were—and his writings are as lively and interesting today as they were in his day—his scheme did not work. Legislators make mistakes; the statutes they pass contain ambiguities; statutes sometimes conflict with one another; and the certainty of statutes has turned out to be an illusion. Even if we look at a dense and comprehensive piece of legislation—the Internal Revenue Code—we find sections of extreme complexity that are almost impossible to interpret. What looks like a detailed prescription for taxing everything the government can think of turns out to befuddle even the officials who are supposed to scrutinize tax returns. Or look at any of the massive sets of regulations in any law library. Any given building in any given city at any given time is undoubtedly in violation of hundreds of building codes. There probably is no one who can identify what all of these violations are or access the appropriate language in the appropriate regulations and codes. We get by because city officials don't have the time or the money to track down every possible violation.

What if officials somehow were able to memorize, internalize, scrutinize, and enforce all existing regulations? That wouldn't work either. Several years ago the New York police went on "strike" by deliberately enforcing every traffic regulation on the crowded Long Island Expressway. They ticketed motorists for every infraction: failing to signal when changing lanes, driving one mile per hour above the speed limit, driving too slowly on an expressway, driving too close to the car in front, passing on the right, failing to give the right of way to automobiles on the entrance ramps, and so forth. There was a great public outcry. While much of the public wrath was directed against the police tactic of calling attention in this manner to their union and their wage demands, the public understood quite well the fact that the rigid laws on the books required discretion and common sense in their enforcement. By acting mechanically and rigidly, the police actually failed to do their assigned job of law enforcement.

The preceding examples incorporate the rules on the law books as one set of factors, and real-world actions as another set. But there's yet another way that legal systems can go awry—the actual invention and creation of new situations that would not have existed but for the presence of certain rules on the books. Tax shelters are a prime example. Taxpayers have found it possible, on the advice and ingenuity of their tax attorneys, to create new situations that seem to fall exactly within the language of the internal Revenue Code yet lead to results that are totally at variance with the purpose of that Code. Many tax shelters have been created that fit exactly the provisions of certain sections of the Internal Revenue Code, but escape taxation. These sheltered situations would never have sprung into existence but for the stimulation provided by the tax laws. In response, some courts have begun to impose a "business purpose" rule on these shelters, saying that if they are created for no purpose other than to comply exactly with the tax code and thus avoid taxation—in short, if they have no real business purpose—then they are taxable anyway. Thus, even if you comply 100% with the statute the way Bentham hoped everyone would, a court might deny you the statutory protection you thought you had achieved.

Truth is stranger than fiction, and the real world is stranger than the laws that try to keep up with it. Situations always arise that are outside the contemplation of the lawmakers. Even if legislators were uniformly as intelligent as Bentham himself, they would not be able to foresee the diverse and ingenious real-world "tests" of their legislation.

Thus, creating ever denser and tighter codes and regulations is not a practical way of governing by rule of law. The more complex the regulations, the more courts will be called upon to interpret them. And judges have no better inherent ability to understand complex regulations than lawyers or legislators; hence even when acting in good faith a court may fail to ascertain what the legislature wanted simply because the legislature said too much on the subject.

2. Austin's Solution

A contemporary critic of Bentham took a quite different view. John Austin charged that legislators are negligent and lack the intelligence and capacity to write comprehensive laws that are free from gaps and ambiguities. Yet Austin was a positivist; indeed, he and Bentham are considered the fathers of positivism. Bentham and Austin were the major positivist theorists of the nineteenth century, they were both unabashed utilitarians, and they both agreed that law is a command backed by a sanction. But on the question of courts, their view diverged sharply.

Austin saw that the role of courts could not be just that of applying statutes, because there were gaps between statutes, ambiguous holes within statutes, and new situations coming up all the time in daily life that were totally unanticipated by past legislators who wrote the statutes. Austin would not have been at all surprised, if he were alive today, at the judicial problems created in lawsuits involving surrogate mothers, a scientific development wholly unanticipated by any legislature. We always seem to have new kinds of cases that are not covered by statute.

Austin's solution was to say that judges of course make up plenty of law; they are, in fact, legislators. Thus, Parliament legislates in broad, sweeping terms; and courts legislate on narrow points in the gaps between statutes or to clarify ambiguities. Austin's approach, therefore, falls in line with Bishop Hoadley's insight. Not only are courts more powerful than legislatures because they interpret legislation, but Austin adds that courts are themselves mini-legislatures.

Austin's solution violates the functional differences between legislatures and courts that I talked about earlier. That in itself would be trivial; Austin is entitled to theorize any way he wants to. But here's what happens when the functional difference is violated. A litigant loses a case in court, and the judge explains why the litigant lost. The judge, using Austin's theory, explains to an accident victim that since no statute directly covered her case, the judge simply legislated some new law that absolves the defendant from paying damages. But the litigant is outraged by this explanation. "You were supposed to apply the law as it was when the accident occurred," she says, "and not invent it now out of whole cloth. To legislate now, when the accident occurred a year ago, is to legislate retroactively. It is totally unfair to me."

The force of this argument, I believe, is why Austin's theory that judges are mini-legislators has largely been rejected. There are many people today who say that, realistically, judges legislate. To this extent, there are Austinians among us. But their theory is no better than Austin's. However, there is a contemporary theorist who attempted to offer a synthesis between Bentham's and Austin's theories in order to explain the law-finding or law-making role of the court. His theory is worthy of careful consideration.

3. Hart's Version of Positivism

The late Professor H.L.A. Hart taught law at Oxford University. Hart's theory is that every word in a statute, as well as the statute as a whole, consists of a core and a penumbra. The core meaning of a word is that which the word clearly signifies; it is entirely unproblematic, definitive, and denotative. For instance, the word "vehicle" in the statute, "All vehicles shall stop at the red light," clearly applies to automobiles and trucks. Hart would say that there is just no way that the driver of an automobile or a truck could argue that his vehicle is not covered by the terms of the statute. However, every word also has a penumbra, a shaded area of meanings within which reasonable people could disagree whether the word covers any of those meanings. Taking the same example, does "vehicle" include bicycles? Motorized wheelchairs? Skateboards? Baby carriages? How about a helicopter that is flying very close to the road; is it a "vehicle" that has to stop and hover just above the red light? In some cities such as Boston there are intersections where all the lights turn red (and yellow) at once, stopping all traffic and allowing the public to cross the intersection in any direction. Would the word "vehicle" apply to bicycles or motorized wheelchairs in Boston, so that they can only cross the intersection when the automobiles and trucks cross, or does it not apply to bicycles and motorized wheelchairs so that they can cross the intersection when all the pedestrians cross it? Hart says that it is very hard to find the answer to these questions in the statute, because these examples come within the penumbra and not the core of the statute.

As a positivist, Hart believes that law consists of commands by the legislature. The command is expressed in a statute. The statute has two parts: a core and a penumbra. The core is a direct, irrefutable, clear command. Hart says that a court has no discretion with respect to the core of the statute. If something is an automobile, then it is a vehicle, and hence it falls within the core of the statute about vehicles. A court must apply the statute regulating vehicles at red lights to the automobile. A court cannot exempt an automobile from the statute because it's a Cadillac or a Mercedes; any make or model of car comes within the core of the statute, and that's it. To this extent, Hart completely agrees with Bentham.

But what about the second part of the statute? Hart says that the court is free to decide what instances come within this second part, or penumbra, of the statute. Thus if a judge wants to decide that a motorized wheelchair is a vehicle for the traffic-control statute, the judge has the discretion to make that decision. Indeed, Hart says that the legislature has delegated to the judge the discretion to make that decision.

Thus Hart's theory of the penumbra is that it is a command to a judge saying, in effect, "you decide what comes within the penumbra. We are giving you legislative power to make that decision—but only as to the penumbra, not as to the core." So in this respect, Hart agrees with Austin.

Thus Hart has split the difference between Bentham and Austin. He agrees with Bentham's idea of total legislative control over courts, but only as to the core portion of a statute. And he agrees with Austin's idea of total court control over legislation, but only as to the penumbral portion. Only Hart doesn't put it the way Austin does. Instead of speaking of court control over the legislature, he theorizes that it is the legislature that has delegated partial legislative competence to the court. It is the legislature, under Hart's theory, that has made the court into a mini-legislature with respect to the penumbra, and the penumbra only.

Let's consider the court's mini-legislative power to interpret the penumbra. What if two courts disagree with each other? What if one judge decides that a motorized wheelchair has to cross with the automobiles, and another judge decides that it has to cross with the pedestrians? We'd have real confusion at that intersection in Boston. (As a matter of fact, there is always real confusion at any intersection in Boston.)

But positivism has no room for any such confusion. Indeed, we can logically derive from positivism the answer to the question of judges differing on the issue whether a wheelchair is a vehicle. Remember that the legislature has delegated legislative power to the judge to make decisions in the area of the penumbra. This means that the very first judge to deal with the motorized wheelchair case will be legislating within the area of the penumbra. Thus, if in that first case the judge decides that a motorized wheelchair is not a vehicle in the traffic-control statute, that decision constitutes a legislative determination—although we can call it a "judicial precedent." All future judges will be bound by the decision in the first case just as if the legislature itself had put it in the statute. All future judges are bound to follow precedent. So there won't be any disagreement among judges about motorized wheelchairs. Under Hart's theory, it is only the *first* judge who gets to exercise the mini-legislative competence.

Of course, we're talking about the first judge with respect to any given interpretation of the penumbra. Thus, even though we've had a "wheelchair" precedent, another case, that of "bicycles," also has to be initially interpreted. If the first judge to get the bicycle case decides that a bicycle is a "vehicle" within the meaning of the traffic-control statute, from then on bicycles have to stop at red lights or be subject to the statutorily prescribed penalties. The word "vehicle" in the statute takes on the additional meaning "including bicycles."

You can see how the legislature would be quite happy with this approach. A legislature can use any words it wants in the statute. If it wants to make a list, such as motorcycles, scooters, horses, and hydrofoils—as well as automobiles, buses, trucks, and bicycles—it can certainly do so. Then all of these vehicles would become part of the "core" of a lengthy statute. On the other hand, the legislature may simply not want to expend the time necessary to think about all these possibilities. In that case they simply write a statute using the word "vehicles" and leave it up to the court to fill in the penumbra. Then, if the legislature is ever dissatisfied with a judicial interpretation—for example, if the legislature feels that motorized wheelchairs should not have been excluded by the judge—the legislature can amend the statute and plug in the term "motorized wheelchairs." Of course, that would only have prospective effect; it can't relate back to the first motorized wheelchair case that was previously decided. But the inability to legislate retroactively is a very small price to pay from the legislature's point of view, because if it ever really cared about—or even thought about—any particular penumbral application, it could have mentioned it explicitly in the statute in the first place.

On the other hand, courts are bound by the precedent laid down by the first judge. So it is not entirely accurate to say that Hart regards courts in general as mini-legislatures. Only the first court to get a particular problem of application has mini-legislative competence; all subsequent courts are bound by the first court's decision. In this respect courts are quite unlike legislatures, for it is a universal feature of statutory legislation that subsequent legislatures are not at all bound by existing statutes; they can revise them at their pleasure.

Hart's position therefore is an intriguing attempt to solve the question of allocation of power between legislature and court. It gives the legislature overwhelming power; the courts must do exactly what the legislature says. It gives the courts only delegated legislative powers in the penumbral areas, which perhaps are those areas where the legislature did not feel it was worth the bother to specify more comprehensively what the statute should cover. But does Hart's analysis really work?

D. CRITICISM OF POSITIVISM

Let's revisit the word "vehicle" in the traffic control statute. Under Hart's theory, a court has absolutely no discretion when the vehicle is an automobile or a truck, because these come within the core meaning of the statute. But now suppose that the automobile is a special kind of automobile—a police car. Suppose the truck is one particular variety of truck—a fire engine. Must all these vehicles stop at the red light? Hart's theory absolutely compels an affirmative answer, because to Hart they are "automobiles" and "trucks" and hence must come under the term "vehicles." Courts would have no discretion to hold to the contrary.

Now you might say that in the real world these cases don't come up, because the police aren't going to arrest themselves for going through a red light, and they aren't going to stop fire engines. But if you look hard enough, the real world will surprise you. One of the fascinating features about law is that you can almost always find a case on just about anything. And so here is a case about fire engines going through red lights.

The case came up in London.[1] Fire engines routinely went through red lights and the police never stopped them for it. But then the members of a union, the Fire Brigade Union, brought a lawsuit to force the drivers of fire engines to stop at the red signal. The union said that it was a dangerous practice for their members to be on fire trucks that went through red lights, and besides their members did not want to violate the law. The chief officer of the London Fire Brigade replied that the union's position was absurd; the duty to put out the fire transcended the obligation to stop at traffic lights. But the union was able to cite in its favor the exact words of the statute, the terms of which applied to any "person driving or propelling a vehicle."

This is a problem for positivism. According to Hart, the core of the statute is perfectly clear; it admits of no exceptions. All that the judge has to do is to determine whether the fire engine is a vehicle. The answer is clearly yes. Therefore, the vehicle must stop at the red light. This is an extremely literal reading of the statute. It is literal

[1] Buckoke v. Greater London Council, 2 All England Reports 254 (1971) (Court of Appeal, Civil Division).

because Hart does not want to give judges any leeway in overriding the legislature; he is concerned about Bishop Hoadley's observation, and wants to make sure, at least in the core cases, that judges have absolutely no discretion. And so in the core instances, positivism is like a computer program; the programmer puts in the commands, and the computer, like a judge in a court, literally obeys the commands without exception. It's also like the curved spikes at the entrance to the parking lot; every vehicle that runs on tires, without exception, will have its tires punctured if it tries to exit over those spikes. Positivism is the theory of curved spikes.

But then doesn't positivism strike you as a rather primitive view of what communication is all about? If the legislature is trying to communicate with the court, the court does not serve the legislature well by taking every word literally. If we look at the statute reasonably, we can't really think that the legislature meant that police cars, fire engines, and ambulances must stop at every red light. Of course, maybe the question of fire engines and ambulances never occurred to the legislators when they put the word "vehicle" in the statute. You'll find in the law that millions of possibilities never occurred to millions of legislators when they drafted millions of statutes. Life is simply too rich and complex for legislators to envisage all the weird situations that can come up if statutes are applied literally.

So, how did the British court handle the fire-engine case? The judge looked through all the statutes, but found that they were no help. There was one statute specifically exempting police cars, ambulances, and fire engines from obeying the *speed limit,* but there was no similar exemption with respect to *traffic signals.* The firefighters union was therefore able to argue, "The idea about fire engines and ambulances did in fact occur to the legislature. We know they thought about fire engines and ambulances because they specifically exempted those vehicles from obeying speed limits. Thus, the legislature must have specifically decided *not* to exempt fire engines with respect to traffic signals. And if the legislature meant to include fire engines in the traffic signal regulations, then what right does a court have to exclude them?"

But the court was realistic too. The court knew that different statutes are enacted at different times, and that the legislature in thinking about fire engines when it enacted one statute wasn't necessarily thinking about fire engines when it enacted a different statute.

The court also must have reasoned that if it adopted a strictly positivistic approach, the result would be that fire engines would stop at red lights, there would be deaths from fires that the engines did not get to fast enough, the public would yell and scream about the absurdity of the law, and Parliament eventually would pass a statute exempting fire engines from stopping at red lights. The court saw no reason to render a decision that Parliament would have to correct later. The court saw no reason to contribute to deaths resulting from fires until the public got so exasperated with the absurdity of the result that they would put pressure on their representatives to correct the statute in the next Parliamentary session. Indeed, we can speculate that the court itself did not want to look foolish in the eyes of the public.

Yet the court had no theory to counteract the positivist theory. The court wanted to support the fire chief's position that fire engines can "shoot the lights." But it did not know how to justify its result.

What did the court do? It simply failed to come up with a reason. It said that it was grafting an exception on to the strictness of the law so as to mitigate its rigor. It also expressed a wish, in the official opinion of the court, that Parliament should amend the law. The court said, "By making the traffic-signal rule an offense without exceptions, Parliament has opened the way to endless discussion in fire stations." The court was obviously bothered by the idea of firefighters endlessly debating the law.

Legal philosophy ought to do better than that. An alternative to positivism should be found. For courts will always be uneasy if they have no justification to back up their decisions. And while the Fire Engine Case came out the sensible way, other cases involving other literal interpretations of statutes might not come out sensibly, in the absence of a good theory of justification.

Because British courts have so thoroughly absorbed the positivist philosophy that has largely been an English contribution to jurisprudence, the court in the Fire Engine Case decided to hand down an unprincipled decision. But that path is a dangerous one. If the courts can "graft an exception" onto the law in the Fire Engine Case, they can do so in all cases. The result would be to vindicate Bishop Hoadley with a vengeance! And it certainly wouldn't make Hart very happy.

But in a way it's Hart's own fault. His theory of the core and the penumbra leads to absurd results because it requires literal interpretation of the "core" parts of statutes. More than that, his theory is essentially an empty one in that it is not itself based on reason or reasonableness but rather upon the dictates of words. The enactment of a statutory word, like the emplacement of curved spikes in front of a parking lot, is merely a brute fact. Such a theory of law fails to be persuasive because it does not, and cannot, take into account the nuances of human personality, the varieties of human conduct, and the legitimate purposes people may have in doing the things that they have to do.

Yet positivism is the dominant Anglo-American theory of jurisprudence. You will find that its influence in the law is pervasive. I've tried in this Chapter to get down to the core meaning of positivism, and to show that it is, ultimately, a failure. But we learn a great deal in finding out exactly how and why it is a failure. On the basis of what we have learned in attacking positivism, we can lay the foundations for an alternative approach to the law.

In Chapter 4 we will look at an alternative to positivism. But I want to end the present Chapter by mentioning a solution to the London fire-brigade case that did not occur to any of the lawyers for the union or the fire chief, or to the English court, or to anyone who has commented on this case in the law journals. What is remarkable about this solution is that it is a solution *within* positivistic theory. The person who came up with it was a student in my class in Jurisprudence at Northwestern Law School in 1987. On the final exam, I summarized the facts of the Fire Brigade Case and the various English statutes and asked if anyone could find a solution within positivist theory. In her exam answer, Deborah Maisel cited the statute that specifically exempted fire engines from speed limits. So, she reasoned, fire engines did not have to obey any speed limits at all. But isn't a traffic signal a form of speed limit? Doesn't the traffic signal mean that you must reduce your speed to zero miles per hour? Ms. Maisel argued that we should interpret the red traffic signal as a speed-limit regulation that imposes a zero speed on all traffic for the duration of the red light. Since fire engines are exempted from obeying speed limits, they can proceed at a speed in excess of zero miles per hour through the red traffic signal!

CHAPTER 4. WHAT IS COURT-MADE LAW?

A. DEFINITION OF LAW AS A PREDICTION

In Chapter 3 we saw some of the things that went wrong with the positivist definition of law. To point the way toward an alternative view of law, I'd like to begin with what I think is the most accurate definition of law, and then defend that definition: Law is a prediction of what courts will decide. Or as Justice Oliver Wendell Holmes put it, "The prophecies of what the courts will do in fact, and nothing more pretentious, are what I mean by the law." The definition is associated with the school of thought known as legal realism.[1]

Suppose you ask a lawyer whether a person you want to call a "liar" can sue you for defamation. You would not be happy if the attorney hands you eight thick volumes on the law of defamation and says that the law is somewhere inside. Nor would you be edified if the lawyer produces a thin volume on "calling people liars." You would still want to know whether, *in your particular case,* the person you name can successfully sue you. A good lawyer, after doing the law research, would simply tell you what your chances are. If the lawyer tells you that in your particular case on your particular facts and on what you can prove about the person you want to call a liar, you have a 90% chance of winning in court, then you will have learned something of value. If you don't want to risk the 10% chance

[1] Many legal realists, for example Karl Llewellyn, use a more expansive view of law: what officials do about disputes is the law itself. "Officials" in this formula include sheriffs, clerks, the police, and lawyers, as well as judges. But the problem with this definition is that courts can review the acts of officials. If you are beaten up in a police station, you have the possibility of going to court and suing the police for violating the law. But if Llewellyn were right the law is what officials do, then the beating administered to you by the police would constitute the law itself and you would have no basis for complaining about it in a court.

that you would lose a legal action against you for defamation, then you won't go ahead and call that person a liar.

Now this may seem straightforward, but many people are bothered by the idea of expressing the content of law as a probability. They want to know *whether or not* calling that person a liar is actionable. They expect the "law" to be a yes-or-no statement. They would want to know, for example, whether the fire engine must legally stop at the red light or whether it may legally ignore the red light. They don't like probabilities.

Because they *assume* that the law is a matter of yes or no, they will interpret the lawyer's estimate of 90% as reflective of the lawyer's degree of ignorance about the law! They would say, "if you really knew what the law was, you wouldn't be giving us a guess or a percentage." Yet they would be wrong, because law can never be certain.

Let me give an example of a law that one might think was 100% certain. My son came home with two traffic tickets. He was charged with going through a stop sign and with speeding. The same officer had ticketed him for going through the stop sign and for speeding. I asked him if he did those things and he said yes. But if he pleaded guilty to both of them, he would have his license suspended, and he needed the car to drive to school. His license wouldn't be suspended if he was convicted of only one of the charges. So I said I would go to court and defend him.

Before the case came up in the crowded traffic court, I talked with the prosecutor. I pointed out to her that my son would lose his license, that the infractions were not serious, and that we would be willing to plead guilty on one of the two offenses if the state would drop the other one. "Nothing doing," she said.

As I thought about the situation, I knew that my case was a loser on the facts as well as on the law. My son had gone through the stop sign, and he also drove faster than the speed limit. The stop sign was a valid stop sign, and the speed limit was a valid speed limit. One might say that on either of these two charges, there was 100% certainty of conviction for traffic violations.

The judge took up the "failure to stop at a stop sign" violation first. He asked me how I would plead for my client, and I replied "not guilty."

The prosecutor then swung into action. She asked the arresting officer a series of questions. He explained that he saw my son's car fail to stop at the stop sign, what the date and time of the offense were, the community in which it occurred, and so forth. Then it was my turn. I asked the policeman whether he was also the arresting officer for the speeding offense, which was coming up next, and he replied that he was. Then I said,

"Did you turn on your siren and Mars lights as soon as my son went through the stop sign?"

He said, "no, not right away."

"In fact," I said, "you kept your distance and followed him for a while, waiting to see whether he would commit any more violations, and in fact he started to speed, and then you turned on your siren and stopped him, right?"

"Yes, that's what I did," he said.

"But if he violated the stop sign, wasn't it your duty to arrest him right then and there, and not wait and see whether he would do something else that was illegal?"

At this point the judge interrupted with words that I was glad to hear: "I'm dismissing this charge. If there was an infraction, the officer should have acted. The officer did not act, and therefore lost the opportunity to arrest the driver for the stop sign violation. The next charge is speeding. How do you plead?"

"Guilty," I said.

We paid the fine and my son got his license back. There was no doubt whatsoever that he had violated the stop sign, and yet any prediction of certainty that he would be convicted for it would have been wrong.[2]

Law is a matter of probabilities the same way that the basic constituents of the universe—electrons, protons, neutrons, quarks, leptons, muons, and so forth—exist only as probabilities. Quantum theory has shown that we cannot ascertain the exact position and momentum of these elements that make up all matter. Heisenberg's "uncertainty principle" reflects the fundamentally probabilistic na

[2] What about a prediction that it was 100% certain that my son would have been convicted on the second charge, that of speeding? After I left the courtroom, an argument occurred to me that might have also acquitted my son on the second charge! Can you figure out what that argument would be?

ture of our universe. I mention this to say that law is in good company when we call the law uncertain.

Before the quantum theories were established in the late 1920s, Einstein had speculated that the probabilities assigned to quantum events were simply a measure of the observer's ignorance. For instance, it may be observed that there is a 10% chance of an orbiting electron being found outside the potential energy sphere of a hydrogen atom (proton). Einstein felt that the electron was either inside or outside the potential energy sphere, and only human ignorance and the crude limits of our macroscopic measuring devices stood in the way of determining the precise location of the electron. But quantum theory disproved the Einsteinian analysis. We now know that the individual electron's position is in fact and by its nature indeterminate, and that its real position is precisely calibrated by a probability function. Thus the 10% figure actually measures the location of an individual electron; the electron is somehow 10% outside the potential energy sphere and 90% inside. This is impossible to visualize if we think of the electron as a particle, but the electron isn't quite a particle, it's a wave-particle. If we were to make aggregate statistical measurements, we would find that roughly 10% of all electrons of hydrogen atoms are located outside the sphere. But the intellectual challenge of quantum theory consists of the fact that what statistically is true of an aggregate of electrons is somehow also true of an individual electron.

You don't need to understand quantum theory to understand law, but I do want to point out that what seems mysterious or strange about the prediction theory of law is actually analogous to the microscopic constituents of matter in the real world. Thus when the attorney says that your chance of winning is 90%, that is an *exact* number. It does not mean that the attorney is only 90% sure of what the law is. It means that the attorney is 100% sure of what the law is, and the law itself is a 90% probability.

One might object that at least any case that has actually been decided is crystal clear; the law is exactly what that case said it was. Even this is analogous to quantum mechanics: we can tell with certainty where an electron was by looking at the path it traced in a Wilson cloud chamber. But we cannot tell with certainty where an electron *is* any more than we can tell with certainty what the law *is.* A case that was decided last year, then, is a measurement of what the law was a year ago. At the time the case was argued, the law could only be expressed as a probability. But once the court decided the case, then the law became a past fact. That past fact cannot determine what the law will be in the future; even a clear judicial precedent can be "overruled." Moreover, no case is exactly like any past case. If you want to know whether you can get away with calling someone a liar, you might read 100 "liar" decisions but they cannot tell you with certainty about your own case. After all, the person you want to call a liar is not the same person as the cast of characters in those 100 previous cases, the facts are not exactly the same, the circumstances are different, and so on. There is, and must be, an element of legal uncertainty in any case.

One might well ask why in some cases the legal uncertainty is so high. An attorney might say that your chances of winning are 40% or 50%, and right away you think that you could have flipped a coin and gotten the same result. But very few situations out of the thousands of everyday law situations that we encounter have such a high degree of indeterminacy as 50%. Most of the time, when the law is as highly determinate as 99%, people simply don't ask attorneys about it. You don't need to ask an attorney to interpret a stop sign for you. You know that if you're driving a car and fail to stop at the stop sign, there is more than a 99% chance that you've committed a traffic violation (and you could be arrested if a police officer sees it). Attorneys get most of their business in the areas of lower predictability, where the law isn't clear.

In addition, there are some laws that always seem indeterminate. Consider the laws against "vagrancy" or being a "public nuisance." These are very hard to define, and yet we seem to recognize clear cases when they occur. But there is a more general point to be made about indeterminate laws, and that is, the closer you look at *any* law the more indeterminate it becomes "around the edges." Consider the "clear" law of stopping at a stop sign. What constitutes a "stop"? Is a "rolling stop" a stop? If you observe any given stop sign, you will see some cars come close to stopping but never stop; others will clearly stop; a few might simply slow down a little. The degree of variability between slowing down and stopping is so great that it would be impossible to specify exactly what constitutes stopping in those borderline cases. A police officer might or might not arrest someone for making a "rolling stop," and that person might or might not be able to convince the traffic court judge that it was truly a stop.

Since all laws are necessarily indeterminate, and since the very best lawyers will always speak of the law in percentage probability terms, why are lawyers so highly paid in our society? It may seem paradoxical, but the general success of lawyering as a profession has a lot to do with the fact that any client's situation can only be assessed in terms of probabilities and not certainties. Consider: a lawyer tells you that your chances of winning the previously mentioned "liar" case are 90 out of 100. Suppose the case is filed, you hire that lawyer, and you lose the case. You confront him with his prediction of 90% and he replies, "exactly right; you had a 10% chance of losing and, unluckily for you, you lost." *No* prediction of the outcome of a case can ever itself be *falsified.* Just as you can bet on all the red and black outcomes of the spin of a roulette wheel and still lose because the ball improbably lands on the green number, so too any assertion of law has a finite probability of either prevailing or being defeated. In short, in any single given case, a lawyer cannot be wrong! And that, I submit, has a lot to do with the success of the profession as a whole.

But I'm not saying that some lawyers aren't better than others. A lawyer who loses a *series* of 90% cases perhaps should go into a different line of work. Even though an attorney's reputation cannot be broken (or made) as the result of a single case, how well the lawyer does over a range of cases is indeed the determinant of the lawyer's reputation. The situation is not qualitatively different from the meteorologist on television. The weatherperson might predict an 80% chance of sunshine tomorrow, and yet the next day there is a downpour. No problem; there was after all a 20% prediction of rain, and that's what occurred. So we "forgive" the bad weather prediction. However, if we observe over the course of several weeks that most of the above 50% predictions by that meteorologist turn out to be wrong, we will consider switching to a different channel. ("I always watch channel 7; they give better weather.")

1. Subjective Probability?

I have been trying to defend a wholly objective definition of law as a prediction of judicial decisions. Let me suggest four problems with my approach and try to deal with those problems. First—and this is a fairly recondite problem—every prediction of what a court will decide is, of course, a prediction of a unique event. The facts in any given case can never be exactly the same as the facts in any other case (at minimum, the *time* that the facts occurred has to be different). Thus, a lawyer's percentage prediction of the result of a judicial decision must be, like a meteorologist's, the prediction of a one-time event. Sometimes this is called, in the mathematical literature, "subjective probability." Our first problem, then, is how can I reconcile my "objective" view of law when it depends on something called "subjective probability"?

The term "subjective probability" was coined in order to distinguish it from the notion of probability over many occurrences of the same thing. Probability originally was conceived as the number of times a certain event would occur out of a long run of similar events, such as the number of times heads would come up if you tossed a coin a thousand times.[3] But if you toss a new coin once, a coin that has never been tossed before, advocates of the "long run" probability notion say that you can only measure your *degree of confidence* that the coin has a 50% chance of coming up heads, and this is called "subjective probability." It is based, they say, on one's ignorance of the true factors (wind currents, gravity, molecular motion, energy imparted to the toss itself, the angle of toss, and so forth) that determine how the coin is going to come up.

Even if these advocates of "subjective probability" are correct about a unique coin toss event—and so far there's no consensus among mathematicians about this—my model for law is not like this "subjective probability" notion, but rather is analogous to quantum theory where the individual event being predicted is itself spread over a range of probabilities. In my definition of law, as in quantum

[3] One of the earliest philosophers of probability, the great mathematician Poisson, actually used for much of his data the outcomes of numerous civil lawsuits in the French courts.

theory, the probability is not at all subjective. It is not a measure of the degree of the observer's ignorance. Rather, it is an exact measure of the degree of indeterminacy of the thing being measured.

2. Self-Prediction by Judges?

A second problem, somewhat building upon my answer to the first one, has proved to be a real mind-twister. It may be presented in the following question: If law is a prediction of what courts will decide, how can my theory of law be used by a judge? A judge needs to know what the law is. If a judge uses my theory to decide what the law is, doesn't that require him to predict what a judge would decide? More pointedly, doesn't it require him to predict what he himself is going to decide? If the answer is yes, doesn't that leave him total discretion to decide anything he likes on the ground that such a decision is exactly what he predicted he would decide?

Let's put this question into concrete terms that could come up in the course of a legal argument. If the judge asks you what is the law in your case, and an attorney responds, "your honor, the law is whatever you predict you will decide," then my definition would break down. It would fall into a paradox of self-reference. More than that, it would become totally subjective, depending upon the whims of the judge. However, the fallacy lies in the attorney's response. She should not have responded in that manner.

The attorney should have responded to the judge's question as follows, "your honor, the law is what you would predict a judge would decide who knew as much as you do about the facts of this case." And the judge then asks, "What judge—me?" The attorney replies: "Not necessarily. I am talking about the average judge sitting in the courts of this jurisdiction, which includes your honor to the extent that you participate in this average."

"How can I possibly predict what an average judge would decide if I'm one of the judges that make up the average?"

"By simply excluding from your deliberations whatever factors might enter into your deliberations that are peculiar to you as an individual that you know about. You should abstract yourself, so to speak, from whatever personal characteristics, or perhaps I could use the term idiosyncrasies, that you might have, and decide the case the way the average judge in this jurisdiction would decide it. The other judges don't have your personal characteristics; each may have his or her own, but all idiosyncracies should cancel out, and you should apply only those thought processes used in deciding cases that you know are common to all of you."

That answer, I submit, contains no circularity nor subjective element. It may not give a judge a clue as to the content of the law (how could any *definition* of law generate *content?*) but it does tell the judge what to exclude. The judge should exclude all biases, prejudices, and idiosyncracies of which the judge is aware.

My suggestion that a judge should decide the case the way an average judge would decide the case coincides with the conclusion that the attorneys on both sides of the case should come up with after they study the law of the case. The attorneys, not knowing which judge will be assigned to their case, must research the law with an eye toward predicting what *any* judge, *any* average judge, might decide. That is the standard the attorneys use, and therefore it should also be the standard the judge uses, because the law as laid down by the judge should not come as a surprise. Law itself may be indeterminate, but when a judge finds what the law is in a given case, that finding should not come as a surprise to the parties. (If it did, then law would hardly be able to channel our conduct, which is its function as I claimed at the beginning of Chapter 1.)

3. Judicial Decisions Based on Probability

But this raises a third problem: what does the judge do when he measures the law according to the definition I have given, and concludes that his best prediction of what a judge would decide in the present case on the present facts is 60% in favor of the plaintiff? The judge only has one decision to make. Does he now have a 40% width of discretion to award the decision to the defendant?

My answer is clearly no. The judge, in this example, has no discretion; he must award the decision to the plaintiff. Picture a judge as deciding on the law the same way a jury decides on the facts. If at the close of a civil case (I'll leave criminal cases out of it because of the higher standard of proof[4]), the jury finds that 51% of the weight of the evidence favors the plaintiff, then the jury should (and is instructed to) award the decision to the plaintiff. For any whole percentage point less than that, the plaintiff has not proven her case and therefore the decision should go to the defendant. Specifically, at 50-50, the weight of the evidence is evenly balanced and therefore the status quo should not be disturbed; the decision should go to the defendant.

This same calculation applies to the judge. If the judge finds that the law is so uncertain that a prediction of what an average judge would decide comes out only to the figure of 51% in favor of the plaintiff, nevertheless the judge should award the decision to the plaintiff invariably and without exception.

But then, you might ask, doesn't this make the law a lot more certain? If an attorney researches the law and finds that it is 60% in the plaintiff's favor, shouldn't the lawyer be 100% confident that the plaintiff will win, and not just 60% confident? No, because the 60% figure represents the attorney's best estimate of what will happen. The attorney cannot be certain that a judge will arrive at the same figure. The degree of the attorney's uncertainty that a judge will arrive at the same figure is, precisely, 60%.[5] As desirable as it would be to make the law in general more certain, the fact is that some law is inherently indeterminate and the best we can do is to allow it to shape our lives as a probability risk factor rather than as a certainty. And maybe this is better. Since we live in a dictatorship of law anyway, it may be preferable to serve under a dictator who is not rigorously and mechanistically determinate.

4. Divergence of Predictions Among Attorneys

In what ways can an attorney be wrong in calculating a figure of, say, 60%? This is our fourth problem in considering the theory of law that I have been advocating. To introduce it, let's again consider a comparison with the meteorologist.

[4] But the mathematics is exactly the same. If the state has to prove beyond, say, 70% that the defendant is guilty, then any proof less than or equal to 70% should result in acquittal.

[5] Indeed, the lawyer's figure of 60% already takes into account, and thus discounts, the ground rule that if the judge finds the figure to be 60% the judge will be certain to rule for the plaintiff.

In our comparison between forecasting the weather and forecasting judicial decisions, consider the following major difference. Suppose the meteorologist on channel 2 predicts that there is an 80% chance of rain tomorrow, and the meteorologist on channel 5 predicts a 60% chance of rain. Both cannot be right. If we find that one prediction is based on a study of satellite photos and reports of weather conditions around the country, and the other is based upon whether a certain stick held in both hands is bent toward the ground at a certain angle, we might have a higher degree of confidence in the first one.

Now compare that situation with two lawyers who give you a prediction whether you're going to win your case against your landlord. Lawyer A says you have an 80% chance of winning, and lawyer B says 60%. Can they both be right? It's possible that, like the meteorologists, one lawyer has studied the problem and the other is simply guessing without doing any research. But let's make it harder by supposing that both lawyers have studied the problem very carefully.

Here's how they can both be right. Lawyer A is an expert in landlord-tenant law. He knows that if he takes your case, he will personally argue the case in court and, on the facts as you have recounted them, he has an 80% degree of confidence in winning. Lawyer B is a securities-law expert. She knows that if she takes your case, she knows so little about landlord-tenant law that, at best, she will have only a 60% chance of winning. Therefore, she is correct in predicting 60%, and lawyer A is correct in predicting 80%. The law is actually different for you depending upon whom you engage to represent you.

Consider the difference between law and quantum theory. In the latter field, two physicists looking at the same data will apply the same formula and come up with the same statistical probabilities. However, two lawyers looking at the same factual data might come up with different estimates of success. In physics, we do not say that the knowledge and personality of the individual physicist can have any effect upon the probability of an electron orbiting outside the usual range of orbit for a hydrogen atom. But in law, we can and do say that the knowledge, personality, ability, and talents of the individual attorney can have a dramatic effect upon the outcome of the case. Defense attorney Perry Mason usually wins and prosecutor Hamilton Burger usually loses. Of course, the author, Erle Stanley Gardner, takes pains to show us that it is not Perry's rhetorical brilliance alone that does the trick, but rather his dogged pursuit of the truth. But even if it's just the latter, the fact remains that a good attorney who will personally track down all the clues and personally read the relevant cases and do the relevant LEXIS searches, would probably have a better chance of winning a case than an attorney who leaves these critical matters to a junior associate in the law firm or, worse, ignores them entirely.

The difference is encapsulated in Mark Twain's lament, "everybody talks about the weather but nobody does anything about it." A meteorologist cannot intervene in the weather to safeguard the accuracy of his prediction. But a lawyer can participate in the very case that she predicts, so as to change the odds. This fact about the legal profession has a creative side and also a darker side. On the creative side, we can say that law is not the cut-and-dried reporting of facts and the mechanical classification of such facts under so-called relevant legal principles. Rather, its outcome depends in large part on who the players are, and one of the chief players is the attorney.

But on the darker side, we must acknowledge that the law can be different depending upon the quality of the lawyers. On the average it means that rich people get a better deal from the law than poor people, because they can afford to hire better lawyers. It means that justice is, to some extent, dependent upon what you can afford to pay for justice. And that is not the way things should be. The legal profession in my opinion is not doing enough collectively to improve the quality of justice for people who cannot afford it. Certainly a vast improvement must be made in the delivery of quality legal services to poor or disenfranchised people. The Hippocratic oath in medicine requires doctors to care for the sick, regardless of whether they can afford it; the legal profession needs a similar commitment to care for the needs of those in legal trouble, irrespective of pay. The ethical principles are there, but there must be a greater willingness to act upon them. The idea of devoting oneself to serve those who need help, in my opinion, is what it really means to be a member of a profession.

B. THE PREDICTIVE THEORY AND POSITIVISM

I've now presented and tried to defend an objective theory of law. How does it relate to the theory of positivism that we discussed in Chapter 3? Specifically, how can a positivist interpret the fact that a lawyer can make a difference in determining what the law is?

1. Indeterminacy of Statutes

There seems to be no room for it in Hart's theory of positivism. We now see that a statute—which the positivists thought was the very definition of law as the command of the legislature—becomes only a partial predictor of judicial decisions. The predictive power of the statute depends on several factors, prominent among which is how close the statute fits the facts of the case. A statute making gambling a crime may directly apply to off-track betting on horses, but does it apply to friendly card games, or to pin-ball machines? Does it apply to investing in the stock market, which many people say is a gamble? Does it apply to accident insurance or medical insurance? Isn't the insurance company gambling on your continued good health? We are getting farther and farther away, in these examples, from the most direct application of the statute to off-track betting on horses. The statute sort of spreads out over these other possible applications, impacting upon them in a glancing manner. I'm not talking here about core and penumbra, which to Hart is a well-defined concept; rather, I'm talking about direct and indirect, about more and less, like a wave front across a spectrum of possibilities. And there will be a lawyer on one side arguing that it's more, and the lawyer on the other side arguing that it's less, and the quality of their arguments and their research and preparation will make a difference.

If we're going to be intellectually rigorous, we will have to conclude that statutes do not mechanistically apply to real-world situations. A statute may be like a computer program, but the real world is not, or at least so far hasn't been, programmable. The real world presents an array of problems, some of which seem to fit the descriptions in certain statutes, some of which fit the statutes only ambiguously, and many of which appear to have nothing to do with any given statute.[6] Since statutes do not dictate results in particular cases, we have to allow some room for the argumentative ability of attorneys.

This argumentative ability that I'm talking about, that can sometimes make a difference in the probability assigned to any given statement of the law, is only one of the kinds of inputs into judicial decision making. It's just a little window that looks beyond positivism into a fuller theory of adjudication. There are other windows, and they may be a lot more important than the argumentative skills of attorneys.

2. Language and Law

Law is a verbal profession. Lawyers deal in words the same way that a botanist deals in plants and an architect deals in blueprints. There are two different ways a person can deal with words. First, she might simply use language to express meanings and not think about language itself at all. Second, she might use language self-reflexively in a kind of simultaneous double awareness of the meaning she has in mind and of the words she uses as an imperfect vehicle for conveying that meaning. My academic career swung like a pendulum back-and-forth between these approaches.

In high school I only used words to convey my thoughts. I did not think much about a word as a vehicle for thought, though I was interested in the expressive use of words (as a young wannabe poet). In college, I started out as an English-and-Lit. major, but soon drifted to the strongest departments that Cornell had in those days, Philosophy and Polysci. I took philosophy classes and became immersed in the ordinary language philosophy of Ludwig Wittgenstein. My professors were among his most prominent students and interpreters—Max Black, Norman Malcolm, and Rogers Albritton. Soon I could hardly read anything without wondering about the semantic content of the words and whether they could capture the intent of the author. I learned that our use of words tends to assume the very thing we are trying to prove; that as soon as we say

[6] This is indeed the fundamental problem with current research in artificial intelligence. How can a computer be designed to recognize things the way a brain does? And if such a computer is eventually achieved, how can it then be made to *evaluate* what it sees?

something we are stating a tautological truth that is an artifact of language and not necessarily a truth about the real world. By my senior year I had so "deconstructed" words and meanings in the Wittgensteinian tradition that I became a total skeptic, disillusioned about the very words we use to communicate. The pendulum had swung back to the opposite extreme from my high school days.

It was disillusionment with language, more than anything else, that led me to decide against going on to graduate school. It was time, I felt, to get out of the ivory tower and into something real—a professional career. Since I had no abiding interest in medicine, architecture, or theology, I decided that I would try the law profession.

I was in for a great surprise. On the first day of law school my teachers seemed to use words in an utterly pragmatic and sensible way—to convey meaning, to refer to things and events in the external world, to talk to us in a most ordinary fashion. It was the way I used to talk before I encountered Wittgenstein. Were my teachers simply ignorant about twentieth century ordinary language philosophy? No, they were very bright and educated people. It's just that they knew that lawyers are in the communications business. Some of them believed that to communicate effectively you cannot afford to get hung up on the meanings of the words you use. Others took the position that each word had a determinate "core" meaning (a position which I believe Wittgenstein refuted.[7])

Here is an example of my early law school experience. In our torts class, Professor John Mansfield took up the word "assault," and looked at it from so many different sides that many of us were frustrated that we could not pin down what "assault" meant. Some of my friends hit the library to figure out what an "assault" is. I was so naive as an entering law student that I had no idea that there were hornbooks or treatises about the law. So when my friends told me that certain books, like *Prosser on Torts,* were helpful to them in making sense of what Professor Mansfield was saying in class, I went to the library and looked into that book. It was the first, and last, time I ever looked into a hornbook or treatise in my three years in law school. For what I found was appalling. Everything that Prosser wrote about "assault"—how it was defined, how it was used, whether the

[7] See, e.g., Saul Kripke, Wittgenstein on Rules and Private Language (1982).

courts were right or wrong in using it one way or the other—struck me as foolish in light of the classroom discussions we had had. My mind was full of Professor Mansfield's meticulous questioning of the meaning of "assault," and I was amazed to see that Prosser's account totally failed to answer any of Professor Mansfield's questions. Indeed, the famous book *Prosser on Torts* seemed to me to be like a second-rate set of law-school notes on Professor Mansfield's class by someone who didn't "get it." So I abandoned the hornbooks and the treatises as not worth my (severely limited law-student) time. I remember thinking that reading a hornbook or a treatise was a form of un-learning.

But that's not the point of my example. For it soon became clear to me that Professor Mansfield was not *deconstructing* the idea of an "assault" the way Wittgenstein might have deconstructed it. Rather, for Professor Mansfield, "assault" was something that exists in the real world. It may be hard for us to figure out what an "assault" is, and we may have to evolve an enormously nuanced definition constructed on the scattered remains of many litigated cases, but nevertheless there surely are things that are "assaults" just as surely as there are other causes of action in the law (like battery, negligence, bills of lading, probable cause) that are not "assaults." So it would seem that Professor Mansfield would not have accepted the notion that "assault" (and all the other words of the law) were essentially tautological.

Soon I found the study of law quite refreshing. No one seemed to be hung up on words. Everyone seemed to think that words actually captured a portion of reality. Reality itself was complex enough for my taste; why make it worse by questioning the language you use? Words, mere words, were just tools that were available to do a lawyer's job.

This practical view of words stayed with me as I began a career in teaching law. I soon found myself thinking that Wittgenstein & Co. were ivory-tower skeptics, out of touch with the real world of business and practical affairs. I felt myself turning into an imperfect copy of my own law professors, using words as tools to get a job done. I become a conduit, outputting to my students the same attitudes that were inputted to me when I was a law student.

But then the pendulum abruptly swung back. I began to do a considerable amount of courtroom litigating—at the pretrial level, at the trial level, and at the appellate level. I met with clients and heard their stories; I met with witnesses and went over their forthcoming testimony; I argued motions before judges; I handled cases at the trial level; I wrote memos, briefs, and motions of all kinds at the trial and appellate levels. And I began to see, as experienced litigators see, that Wittgenstein and Co. had important insights that practicing lawyers cannot afford to ignore. Wittgenstein sensed what litigators know: that words tend to unravel in the crucible of litigation. Words strike different judges in different ways.[8] Any word you use will strike a jury in at least twelve different ways. You can put a sentence together and think that it nails down its own meaning—that its meaning is and must be obvious to all, questionable to none—only to find, later on, that it was entirely, grotesquely, incomprehensibly, radically misinterpreted.[9]

[8] One brief example: I was at a lunch where there were several judges, and the conversation turned to the First Amendment. At the time I had been preparing for an oral argument in the Seventh Circuit Court of Appeals on a case that involved freedom of speech. The particular concept of "chilling effect" was pertinent to my case, as it involved a statute that was okay if applied to a normal case but could exert a chilling effect on free speech generally because of its broad statutory language. So at one point in the conversation, I worked in the term "chilling effect," and the judge across the table practically jumped out of his chair. He said, "There is no such thing as a chilling effect! We decide the cases as they come up on the merits, period. I can't stand that expression 'chilling effect.'" Right then and there I resolved to drop the idea of "chilling effect" in my brief and oral argument in the forthcoming case. Although none of the judges at the lunch served on the Seventh Circuit Court of Appeals, it seemed to me that if one judge hated the expression "chilling effect" so much, maybe one or two of the judges on the panel for my case might feel the same way. As a result, I directly omitted the concept of "chilling effect" from my brief; instead, some of the cases I cited used that concept, and I hoped that maybe the concept could get in through the back door in that indirect fashion. In addition, I never used the expression "chilling effect" in my oral argument. I would have liked to use it, but I was afraid of using it. (Months later I received word by mail that I had won the appeal, and since so many factors enter into a decision, it was possible that one thing that helped me was avoiding the expression "chilling effect".)

[9] Juries are capable of misinterpreting things other than words. In a famous college football case, coach Bear Bryant had signed his name to a key document, and his lawyers triumphantly introduced the document and its signature to the jury. Other copies of Bryant's signature were submitted to prove that Bryant had indeed signed the document in question. The lawyers believed that nothing could be more obvious than the fact that the signature on the document was Bear Bryant's signature.

Now, of course, no one signs in exactly the same way every time. You can try this out by signing your name five times and noting the slight differences in each rendering.

To the utter surprise of the lawyers, the jury reached an adverse verdict by deciding that the signature was forged.

The jurors had studied the signatures intensively in the jury room, and argument raged back and forth as to whether minute differences in the signatures meant that they were not written by the same hand. An engineer among the jurors calibrated the ink strokes and

I am not aware of any human occupation in which the power of words is tested to its limit as much as in the practice of litigating a case. In a trial, words are used as descriptions of events, as names of persons and things, as modes of thought, as includers or excluders of other words ("probative" versus "prejudicial" testimony), as ways of painting a picture of what happened or what you hope the judge and jurors will believe happened, as conveyers of theories, policies, hopes, and fears, and finally, the words that count so much that they swamp all the other words in the case: the words that express the "brute force" of the final decision. Practicing lawyers become experts in the use and abuse of words.

When I begin an oral argument to a three-judge panel, I see before me three robed citizens who appear similar to each other in many respects, especially garment-wise. But inside they have wildly divergent life experiences, and react differently to each word that I utter. Although my words may produce a surface conformity of judicial behavior, the meanings they evoke in each judge can be different. As I make my argument, for all I know the images in the judges' minds may be shaping and misconstruing everything I say. A word that a judge doesn't like, or a bit of body language, might send a judge down an unwanted byroad. No wonder that lawyers dress conservatively in court; you wouldn't want to wear something that might remind a judge of his no-good brother-in-law. Indeed, there is much to be said in favor of the English practice of wearing wigs in court. "Stuffy" though the practice may seem to us, it serves the useful function of depersonalizing lawyers and judges, of calling attention away from the person and toward the merits of the argument.

No matter which words I use in oral argument—nouns, adjectives, legal phrases, names of other judges, case citations—each will evoke for each judge the wholly personal contexts in which that judge has learned that word over time. As Quine so well put it:

"proved" that there were differences. Apparently no one suggested the simple experiment of signing their own names five times and seeing whether the differences weren't just as different as those on the Bear Bryant specimen signatures.

If jurors can do this with signatures, imagine what they can do with words, especially vague and general words like "was the defendant negligent?" or "did the plaintiff exercise due care?"

> Different persons growing up in the same language are like different bushes trimmed and trained to take the shape of identical elephants. The anatomical details of twigs and branches will fulfill the elephantine form differently from bush to bush, but the overall outward results are alike.[10]

When a case decision turns on the meaning of a word, you can bet that good lawyers will look at that word inside and out. This is even true if the word is someone's *name.* Names—as Plato pointed out in his great but neglected dialogue *Cratylus* and Bertrand Russell discussed in his theory of descriptions[11]—seem to attach themselves to real-world objects. Somewhat more problematic than the name given to an object is the "name" given to a class of objects; we call those words "nouns" (this was the particular emphasis of Plato's *Cratylus*). If we look up at the sky at night and observe a star, we may think of the object we see as a very distant, massive, white-hot body undergoing nuclear fusion like our sun. Yet we are only seeing the light that was emitted from that body in the past. The "star" could have emitted the light a hundred million years ago. Fifty million years ago the same "star" could have exploded into a supernova and dissipated its gaseous energy so that today nothing exists in the spot where we "see" a "star." Or, to take an example from the law, consider the noun "person." The law tells us that a corporation is a "person" for purposes of interpreting the word "person" in the Constitution. The law also tells us that a fetus is not a "person." We can say that a fetus is a "potential person" paralleling the way we call a corporation an "artificial person," but if a fetus were really a "person" then abortion would be murder. (And if a corporation were really a person, liquidating it would be murder.) Under U.S. law, in interpreting the Constitution, you'd be on safer ground calling a corporation a "person" than calling a fetus a "person."

[10] Willard V.O. Quine, Word and Object 8 (1960).

[11] Bertrand Russell's famous example was the "morning star" and the "evening star." Centuries ago astronomers regarded the morning and evening stars as two different objects—as do some people today. Yet they refer to the same physical object which, as it turns out, is not a star but rather the planet Venus. The opposite situation has been the subject of a few famous cases over the years: the parties to a contract name a particular thing (like "Peerless," the name of a vessel that was the subject of a contract), only to discover later on, in a lawsuit, that there are *two* entirely different objects having exactly the same name (two boats named "Peerless").

When we move from nouns to adjectives, the range of ambiguity and fuzziness grows even wider. A witness at a trial may say, "I saw a woman of average height leave the store," and another witness may say, "I saw a short woman leave the store." They could both be referring to the same woman. One witness may describe a man as bald, and another describe the same man as having thin hair.

It would be tedious to continue with examples like these, so let us jump to the extreme case: the use of abstract terms. J.D. March has given a notable example. He suggests that we reword the Fifth and Fourteenth Amendments to the U.S. Constitution. The present text provides that no person shall be "deprived of life, liberty or property without due process of law." Professor March says that the true meaning of this phrase is really quite clear. It means "no *w* shall be *x* or *y* without *z,* where *w, x, y,* and *z* can assume any values within a wide range."[12] And so they do, and so lawyers earn their living finding out what the courts have held these terms to mean in specific cases.

I don't think that a word can mean *anything at all.* If anyone holds such a radically skeptical position, that person will find it difficult to communicate with anyone about anything. Yet I don't think that any word has a definite "core" meaning that is indisputable. What, then, is the philosophical basis for finding some shared meaning of words, without embracing "core" determinism?

At the root of our ability to use words is an innate notion of similarity. Had our brains not been equipped to notice the similarity between one thing and another, we would not have been able to develop language in the first place. Without an innate notion of similarity, words would only apply in a one-to-one relationship with physical things, and we would need a name for every object that we encounter. Our language would then consist of millions if not billions of words, each naming an object. We would never be able to learn all the names, much less make intelligible use of them.

It is our innate notion of similarity that enables us to make generalizations about the world. These generalizations enable us to make predictions—predictions that are important to us to plan our

[12] *See* Anthony D'Amato & Arthur J. Jacobson, Justice and the Legal System 12–13 (1992).

activities and to anticipate the plans and responses of others. Let us look at how lawyers make predictions.

If a lawyer can predict that a certain set of real-world events will, if narrated in court, have an eighty percent chance of obtaining a favorable judicial decision for her client, then she is employing an elementary notion of similarity in her ability to make this prediction. She must have mentally compared her client's set of real-world events to other similar sets, and made the prediction that a court will reach a result in her client's case that will not depart from the results in prior cases that involved similarly event-situated litigants.

This idea of similarity is primitive. It does not depend upon any theory about law, upon any policy about judicial decisionmaking, nor even upon language (except to the extent that language helps us in the communication process—soundless movies could do the same thing though less efficiently in most cases).

The ordinary-language philosopher Rudolf Carnap demonstrated the fact that an innate notion of similarity was prior to language and indeed was necessary for language-acquisition. In his masterwork *The Logical Structure of the World,*[13] Carnap posited as the basic unit of his system the erleb—a momentary cross section of the total stream of experience. Erlebs are related to each other by "part identity" and "part similarity."[14] The relationships of erlebs are preverbal; a word is simply a label we learn to attach to erleb relationships that we notice.

The importance of similarities for law study has, of course, been noted long ago. *Reasoning by analogy* is said to be the basic way that we "think like a lawyer." Lawyers are able to make predictions for their clients because of their ability to notice similarities across real-world situations. Of course, similarities are pervasively important, applying in all social situations: the family, the office, in voluntary

[13] Rudolf Carnap, The Logical Structure of the World: Pseudoproblems in Philosophy (trans. 1928 R.A. George, 1967). A brilliant, extended commentary on Carnap's work is Nelson Goodman, The Structure of Appearance 110-189 (3d ed. 1977). For Carnap's brief reply to Goodman, see Paul A. Schilpp (ed.), The Philosophy of Rudolf Carnap 944-47 (1963).

[14] Sections 67 to 93 of Carnap's book contain an informal account of his system, whereas Sections 108 to 120 present a formal statement of it. The erleb (abbreviation for *elementarerlebnisse*) is presented in § 67 and formalized in § 109. If life were a succession of unrelated erlebs, we would not know that we were alive. The fact is that each erleb can be related to preceding erlebs by a "Part Identity" (§ 76) or "Part Similarity" (§ 77) relationship.

organizations. The Similarity Engine (real-world similarities fueled by our inductive expectation that similar situations should yield similar results) keeps society running with a minimum of unfair surprises. The legal system is just a formal example of the workings of a Similarity Engine. By becoming familiar with it, lawyers can make useful predictions to clients.

I would like to think of the previously-mentioned pendulum as almost coming to rest. A good lawyer uses words both as a tool for conveying meanings but also as an invitation to reflect upon their ability and limitations in conveying meaning. This duality of language is the hallmark of a good legal education. Many people do not stop to think about any possible disjuncture between the words they use and the thoughts they have. But if you often ponder whether the words you use capture the full meaning of what you are trying to express, you're on your way to understanding law and becoming a good lawyer.

3. The Function and Force of Judicial Precedent

A very large and well decorated window is the doctrine of judicial precedent. If you are suing your landlord, and a previous case dealt with the same issue as the one you're suing about, the judge in your case will undoubtedly cite that precedent and decide your case the same way as the previous one was decided. We all know about judicial precedent, but as soon as we begin to examine it closely, we find some very intriguing and puzzling questions.

Why do courts feel compelled to follow precedent? One possibility is laziness: the judge says that since a previous court has already looked into this issue, why bother doing it all over again? Another reason is to promote certainty and predictability in the law: if you find that the issues in your case have already been decided in previous cases, you can rely that those previous cases accurately stated "the law." Perhaps a third reason is that judges collectively want to avoid criticism. The more they back each other up, and the more they follow each other's decisions, the less room seems to exist for someone to complain that judges are acting arbitrarily or don't know what they're doing.

On the other hand, blind adherence to precedent can lead to great public criticism of judges. In recent years, many state courts have deliberately overruled nineteenth century precedents that uniformly held that wives cannot sue their husbands for assault and battery. The old cases went on the view that wives had no business going to court complaining about anything their husbands did to them. In recent years, as one court after another has overruled those old precedents, very few people were heard to complain that the courts were abandoning certainty and predictability in the law. Indeed, the courts would have been in for enormous public criticism if they had not overruled the old decisions.

But we often have cases of first impression, where there are no direct precedents on the books. We saw in Chapter 3 that when a case of first impression comes up within what Hart calls the penumbra of a statute, then the first court to deal with it acts as a mini-legislature. Let's consider now whether this Austinian aspect of Hart's theory is persuasive. Suppose a person in a motorized wheelchair is given a ticket in Boston for crossing the intersection with the pedestrians instead of with the automobiles, and the case goes to court; we'll call it Case I. The judge holds that the motorized wheelchair is a "vehicle" under the traffic control statute, and hence the defendant has to pay a fine for violating the statute. Hart's theory is that that decision becomes an authoritative interpretation of the statute, as if the legislature itself had mentioned motorized wheelchairs, and therefore the decision is binding upon all future courts.

Now we have Case II; another person in a motorized wheelchair is ticketed for crossing the same intersection with the pedestrians instead of with the automobiles. The judge asks the person in court, "weren't you aware that a previous ruling in this jurisdiction held that motorized wheelchairs were subject to the vehicular traffic regulations?" and the defendant answers, "Yes, I have seen a story about that case in the Boston Globe." And the judge asks, "Then, why didn't you cross with the traffic?" And the defendant's attorney at this point cuts in and says, "Your honor, the defendant is a handicapped person. His life would be in danger if he tried to cross with the trucks and buses and sports cars."

But the judge says that there is a precedent and the court is bound by precedent. The attorney replies, "Not if the precedent is clearly erroneous. Case I was wrongly decided. Case I jeopardizes the lives of handicapped persons."

Well, since these are hypothetical cases, I am free to invent my own verdicts. I hereby order the judge in Case II to overrule the precedent and decide that a motorized wheelchair is not a "vehicle" within the meaning of the Massachusetts traffic control statute.

If you agree with my preferred solution, then you have to disagree with Hart's theory that the judge in Case I was a mini-legislator. The judge in Case I was simply a judge deciding a case. The judge in Case II was also just a judge deciding a case. What the judge in Case II decided was that the previous judge's decision was in error.

And if this analysis works with penumbral cases like motorized wheelchairs, it should work equally well with core cases like our fire-engine case. If Case III holds that a fire engine has to stop at red lights, Case IV might very well decide that it's ridiculous to have fire engines, on their way to prevent a fire from spreading, stop at stop lights. If so, the judge in Case IV will overrule the precedent of Case III. The English court that I cited in Chapter 3 reached the conclusion that fire engines did not have to stop at red lights, but could come up with no plausible reason; it simply said that it had to mitigate the harsh rigor of the law. And so it carved out an exception for fire engines, but it was an unprincipled exception.

We saw that Hart's theory failed in the fire-engine case. The exact case where the statute must apply, namely, in its core, was one in which it was held not to apply. If all you had was Hart's theory, you'd have to say that it was 100% certain that a fire engine is a vehicle and that it must stop at the red light. But we all know that a court is not likely to go along with that result. Hence, Hart's positivism, in this case at least, would be a very poor guide to our ability to predict a judicial result. And if law is nothing other than a prediction, then Hart's theory of positivism fails to help us determine law itself.

But under the alternate theory that I'm suggesting here, the court simply takes the statute into account as one very important input into its decisional process. For most cases, the traffic-control statute will work pretty well. But where there are other factors which recommend themselves to the court, the statute might possibly be eclipsed in an unusual case.

What are these other factors that might recommend themselves to the court? I mentioned judicial precedent. Like a statute, it is very strong; but also like a statute, there are some cases where the court might overrule a precedent. I also mentioned the persuasive ability of an attorney arguing a case. But now that we're considering it more closely, we begin to see that the attorney has to have some good arguments to be persuasive about. It won't work for the attorney just to have a good courtroom style, clear enunciation of words, and a winning personality. What are the kinds of arguments that work? This is a restatement of my earlier question as to what windows can be opened up to help us predict judicial decisions.

In the next two chapters, we will see an array of legal arguments and strategies all addressed to the resolution of a single fascinating case. You will recognize arguments based upon positivism, legal realism, natural law, and justice. You will see their interplay in a manner that cannot be conveyed by expository writing. For you will see the clash of arguments as positions that judges and decisionmakers take in deciding a case and then attempting to be persuasive about how they've decided it.

My own position is a bias in favor of justice. It comes out in the professors' opinions I recount in Chapter 6. And I will deal with it more directly, as an explicit component of what we mean by "law," in Chapter 7.

CHAPTER 5. THE CASE OF THE SPELUNCEAN EXPLORERS*

There is no better way to study law than to read cases. There is no better way to study legal philosophy than to see how various theories of law address a given problem and in the process clash with each other. Professor Lon L. Fuller achieved all of these objectives in a brilliantly imaginative case that he invented, called *The Case of the Speluncean Explorers.* If there was ever one single thing that could be said to provide the very best introduction to legal philosophy and legal reasoning, it is this case. I am pleased to quote my former teacher's case in its entirety in this Chapter. After you read this Chapter, you find a sequel to the Speluncean Explorers' Case in the next Chapter.

The Case of the Speluncean Explorers
by Lon L. Fuller

IN THE SUPREME COURT OF NEWGARTH, 4300

The defendants, having been indicted for the crime of murder, were convicted and sentenced to be hanged by the Court of General Instances of the County of Stowfield. They bring a petition of error before this Court. The facts sufficiently appear in the opinion of the Chief Justice.

TRUEPENNY, C. J. The four defendants are members of the Speluncean Society, an organization of amateurs interested in the exploration of caves. Early in May of 4299 they, in the company of

Roger Whetmore, then also a member of the Society, penetrated into the interior of a limestone cavern of the type found in the Central Plateau of this Commonwealth. While they were in a position remote from the entrance to the cave, a landslide occurred. Heavy boulders fell in such a manner as to block completely the only known opening to the cave. When the men discovered their predicament they settled themselves near the obstructed entrance to wait until a rescue party should remove the detritus that prevented them from leaving their underground prison. On the failure of Whetmore and the defendants to return to their homes, the Secretary of the Society was notified by their families. It appears that the explorers had left indications at the headquarters of the Society concerning the location of the cave they proposed to visit. A rescue party was promptly dispatched to the spot.

The task of rescue proved one of overwhelming difficulty. It was necessary to supplement the forces of the original party by repeated increments of men and machines, which had to be conveyed at great expense to the remote and isolated region in which the cave was located. A huge temporary camp of workmen, engineers, geologists, and other experts was established. The work of removing the obstruction was several times frustrated by fresh landslides. In one of these, ten of the workmen engaged in clearing the entrance were killed. The treasury of the Speluncean Society was soon exhausted in the rescue effort, and the sum of eight hundred thousand frelars, raised partly by popular subscription and partly by legislative grant, was expended before the imprisoned men were rescued. Success was finally achieved on the thirty-second day after the men entered the cave.

Since it was known that the explorers had carried with them only scant provisions, and since it was also known that there was no animal or vegetable matter within the cave on which they might subsist, anxiety was early felt that they might meet death by starvation before access to them could be obtained. On the twentieth day of their imprisonment it was learned for the first time that they had taken with them into the cave a portable wireless machine capable of both sending and receiving messages. A similar machine was promptly installed in the rescue camp and oral communication established with the unfortunate men within the mountain. They asked to be informed how long a time would be required to release them. The engineers in charge of the project answered that at least ten days would be required even if no new landslides occurred. The explorers then asked if any physicians were present, and were placed in communication with a committee of medical experts. The imprisoned men described their condition and the rations they had taken with them, and asked for a medical opinion whether they would be likely to live without food for ten days longer. The chairman of the committee of physicians told them that there was little possibility of this. The wireless machine within the cave then remained silent for eight hours. When communication was re-established the men asked to speak again with the physicians. The chairman of the physicians' committee was placed before the apparatus, and Whetmore, speaking on behalf of himself and the defendants, asked whether they would be able to survive for ten days longer if they consumed the flesh of one of their number. The physicians' chairman reluctantly answered this question in the affirmative. Whetmore asked whether it would be advisable for them to cast lots to determine which of them should be eaten. None of the physicians present was willing to answer the question. Whetmore then asked if there were among the party a judge or other official of the government who would answer this question. None of those attached to the rescue camp was willing to assume the role of advisor in this matter. He then asked if any minister or priest would answer their question, and none was found who would do so. Thereafter no further messages were received from within the cave, and it was assumed (erroneously, it later appeared) that the electric batteries of the explorers' wireless machine had become exhausted. When the imprisoned men were finally released it was learned that on the twenty-third day after their entrance into the cave Whetmore had been killed and eaten by his companions.

From the testimony of the defendants, which was accepted by the jury, it appears that it was Whetmore who first proposed that they might find the nutriment without which survival was impossible in the flesh of one of their own number. It was also Whetmore who first proposed the use of some method of casting lots, calling the attention of the defendants to a pair of dice he happened to have with him. The defendants were at first reluctant to adopt so desperate a procedure, but after the conversations by wireless related above, they finally agreed on the plan proposed by Whetmore. After much discussion of the mathematical problems involved, agreement was finally reached on a method of determining the issue by the use of the dice.

Before the dice were cast, however, Whetmore declared that he withdrew from the arrangement, as he had decided on reflection to wait for another week before embracing an expedient so frightful and odious. The others charged him with a breach of faith and proceeded to cast the dice. When it came Whetmore's turn, the dice were cast for him by one of the defendants, and he was asked to declare any objections he might have to the fairness of the throw. He stated that he had no such objections. The throw went against him, and he was then put to death and eaten by his companions.

After the rescue of the defendants, and after they had completed a stay in a hospital where they underwent a course of treatment for malnutrition and shock, they were indicted for the murder of Roger Whetmore. At the trial, after the testimony had been concluded, the foreman of the jury (a lawyer by profession) inquired of the court whether the jury might not find a special verdict, leaving it to the court to say whether on the facts as found the defendants were guilty. After some discussion, both the Prosecutor and counsel for the defendants indicated their acceptance of this procedure, and it was adopted by the court. In a lengthy special verdict the jury found the facts as I have related them above, and found further that if on these facts the defendants were guilty of the crime charged against them, then they found the defendants guilty. On the basis of this verdict, the trial judge ruled that the defendants were guilty of murdering Roger Whetmore. The judge then sentenced them to be hanged, the law of our Commonwealth permitting him no discretion with respect to the penalty to be imposed. After the release of the jury, its members joined in a communication to the Chief Executive asking that the sentence be commuted to an imprisonment of six months. The trial judge addressed a similar communication to the Chief Executive. As yet no action with respect to these pleas has been taken, as the Chief Executive is apparently awaiting our disposition of this petition of error.

It seems to me that in dealing with this extraordinary case the jury and the trial judge followed a course that was not only fair and wise, but the only course that was open to them under the law. The language of our statute is well known: "Whoever shall willfully take the life of another shall be punished by death." N.C.S.A. (N.S.) § 12-A. This statute permits of no exception applicable to this case, however our sympathies may incline us to make allowance for the tragic situation in which these men found themselves.

In a case like this the principle of executive clemency seems admirably suited to mitigate the rigors of the law, and I propose to my colleagues that we follow the example of the jury and the trial judge by joining in the communications they have addressed to the Chief Executive. There is every reason to believe that these requests for clemency will be heeded, coming as they do from those who have studied the case and had an opportunity to become thoroughly acquainted with all its circumstances. It is highly improbable that the Chief Executive would deny these requests unless he were himself to hold hearings at least as extensive as those involved in the trial below, which lasted for three months. The holding of such hearings (which would virtually amount to a retrial of the case) would scarcely be compatible with the function of the Executive as it is usually conceived. I think we may therefore assume that some form of clemency will be extended to these defendants. If this is done, then justice will be accomplished without impairing either the letter or spirit of our statutes and without offering any encouragement for the disregard of law.

FOSTER, J. I am shocked that the Chief Justice, in an effort to escape the embarrassments of this tragic case, should have adopted, and should have proposed to his colleagues, an expedient at once so sordid and so obvious. I believe something more is on trial in this case than the fate of these unfortunate explorers; that is the law of our Commonwealth. If this Court declares that under our law these men have committed a crime, then our law is itself convicted in the tribunal of common sense, no matter what happens to the individuals involved in this petition of error. For us to assert that the law we uphold and expound compels us to a conclusion we are ashamed of, and from which we can only escape by appealing to a dispensation resting within the personal whim of the Executive, seems to me to amount to an admission that the law of this Commonwealth no longer pretends to incorporate justice.

For myself, I do not believe that our law compels the monstrous conclusion that these men are murderers. I believe, on the contrary, that it declares them to be innocent of any crime. I rest this conclusion on two independent grounds, either of which is of itself sufficient to justify the acquittal of these defendants.

The first of these grounds rests on a premise that may arouse opposition until it has been examined candidly. I take the view that the enacted or positive law of this Commonwealth, including all of its statutes and precedents, is inapplicable to this case, and that the case is governed instead by what ancient writers in Europe and America called "the law of nature."

This conclusion rests on the proposition that our positive law is predicated on the possibility of men's coexistence in society. When a situation arises in which the coexistence of men becomes impossible, then a condition that underlies all of our precedents and statutes has ceased to exist. When that condition disappears, then it is my opinion that the force of our positive law disappears with it. We are not accustomed to applying the maxim *cessante ratione legis, cessat et ipsa lex* to the whole of our enacted law, but I believe that this is a case where the maxim should be so applied.

The proposition that all positive law is based on the possibility of men's coexistence has a strange sound, not because the truth it contains is strange, but simply because it is a truth so obvious and pervasive that we seldom have occasion to give words to it. Like the air we breathe, it so pervades our environment that we forget that it exists until we are suddenly deprived of it. Whatever particular objects may be sought by the various branches of our law, it is apparent on reflection that all of them are directed toward facilitating and improving men's coexistence and regulating with fairness and equity the relations of their life in common. When the assumption that men may live together loses its truth, as it obviously did in this extraordinary situation where life only became possible by the taking of life, then the basic premises underlying our whole legal order have lost their meaning and force.

Had the tragic events of this case taken place a mile beyond the territorial limits of our Commonwealth, no one would pretend that our law was applicable to them. We recognize that jurisdiction rests on a territorial basis. The grounds of this principle are by no means obvious and are seldom examined. I take it that this principle is supported by an assumption that it is feasible to impose a single legal order upon a group of men only if they live together within the confines of a given area of the earth's surface. The premise that men shall coexist in a group underlies, then, the territorial principle, as it does all of law. Now I contend that a case may be removed morally from the force of a legal order, as well as geographically. If we look to the purposes of law and government, and to the premises underlying our positive law, these men when they made their fateful decision were as remote from our legal order as if they had been a thousand miles beyond our boundaries. Even in a physical sense, their underground prison was separated from our courts and writ-servers by a solid curtain of rock that could be removed only after the most extraordinary expenditures of time and effort.

I conclude, therefore, that at the time Roger Whetmore's life was ended by these defendants, they were, to use the quaint language of nineteenth-century writers, not in a "state of civil society" but in a "state of nature." This has the consequence that the law applicable to them is not the enacted and established law of this Commonwealth, but the law derived from those principles that were appropriate to their condition. I have no hesitancy in saying that under those principles they were guiltless of any crime.

What these men did was done in pursuance of an agreement accepted by all of them and first proposed by Whetmore himself. Since it was apparent that their extraordinary predicament made inapplicable the usual principles that regulate men's relations with one another, it was necessary for them to draw, as it were, a new charter of government appropriate to the situation in which they found themselves.

It has from antiquity been recognized that the most basic principle of law or government is to be found in the notion of contract or agreement. Ancient thinkers, especially during the period from 1600 to 1900, used to base government itself on a supposed original social compact. Skeptics pointed out that this theory contradicted the known facts of history, and that there was no scientific evidence to support the notion that any government was ever founded in the manner supposed by the theory. Moralists replied that, if the compact was a fiction from a historical point of view, the notion of compact or agreement furnished the only ethical justification on which the powers of government, which include that of taking life, could be rested. The powers of government can only be justified morally on the ground that these are powers that reasonable men would agree upon and accept if they were faced with the necessity of constructing anew some order to make their life in common possible.

Fortunately, our Commonwealth is not bothered by the perplexities that beset the ancients. We know as a matter of historical truth that our government was founded upon a contract or free accord of men. The archeological proof is conclusive that in the first period following the Great Spiral the survivors of that holocaust voluntarily came together and drew up a charter of government. Sophistical writers have raised questions as to the power of those remote contractors to bind future generations, but the fact remains that our government traces itself back in an unbroken line to that original charter.

If, therefore, our hangmen have the power to end men's lives, if our sheriffs have the power to put delinquent tenants in the streets, if our police have the power to incarcerate the inebriated reveler, these powers find their moral justification in that original compact of our forefathers. If we can find no higher source for our legal order, what higher source should we expect these starving unfortunates to find for the order they adopted for themselves?

I believe that the line of argument I have just expounded permits of no rational answer. I realize that it will probably be received with a certain discomfort by many who read this opinion, who will be inclined to suspect that some hidden sophistry must underlie a demonstration that leads to so many unfamiliar conclusions. The source of this discomfort is, however, easy to identify. The usual conditions of human existence incline us to think of human life as an absolute value, not to be sacrificed under any circumstances. There is much that is fictitious about this conception even when it is applied to the ordinary relations of society. We have an illustration of this truth in the very case before us. Ten workmen were killed in the process of removing the rocks from the opening to the cave. Did not the engineers and government officials who directed the rescue effort know that the operations they were undertaking were dangerous and involved a serious risk to the lives of the workmen executing them? If it was proper that these ten lives should be sacrificed to save the lives of five imprisoned explorers, why then are we told it was wrong for these explorers to carry out an arrangement which would save four lives at the cost of one?

Every highway, every tunnel, every building we project involves a risk to human life. Taking these projects in the aggregate, we can calculate with some precision how many deaths the construction of them will require; statisticians can tell you the average cost in human lives of a thousand miles of a four-lane concrete highway. Yet we deliberately and knowingly incur and pay this cost on the assumption that the values obtained for those who survive outweigh the loss. If these things can be said of a society functioning above ground in a normal and ordinary manner, what shall we say of the supposed absolute value of a human life in the desperate situation in which these defendants and their companion Whetmore found themselves?

This concludes the exposition of the first ground of my decision. My second ground proceeds by rejecting hypothetically all the premises on which I have so far proceeded. I concede for purposes of argument that I am wrong in saying that the situation of these men removed them from the effect of our positive law, and I assume that the Consolidated Statutes have the power to penetrate five hundred feet of rock and to impose themselves upon these starving men huddled in their underground prison.

Now it is, of course, perfectly clear that these men did an act that violates the literal wording of the statute which declares that he who "shall willfully take the life of another" is a murderer. But one of the most ancient bits of legal wisdom is the saying that a man may break the letter of the law without breaking the law itself. Every proposition of positive law, whether contained in a statute or a judicial precedent, is to be interpreted reasonably, in the light of its evident purpose. This is a truth so elementary that it is hardly necessary to expatiate on it. Illustrations of its application are numberless and are to be found in every branch of the law. In *Commonwealth v. Staymore* the defendant was convicted under a statute making it a crime to leave one's car parked in certain areas for a period longer than two hours. The defendant had attempted to remove his car, but was prevented from doing so because the streets were obstructed by a political demonstration in which he took no part and which he had no reason to anticipate. His conviction was set aside by this Court, although his case fell squarely within the wording of the statute. Again, in *Fehler v. Neegas* there was before this Court for construction a statute in which the word "not" had plainly been transposed from its intended position in the final and most crucial section of the act. This transposition was contained in all the successive drafts of the act, where it was apparently overlooked by the draftsmen and sponsors of the legislation. No one was able to prove how the error came about, yet it was apparent that, taking account of the contents of the statute as a whole, an error had been made, since a literal reading of the final clause rendered it inconsistent with everything that had gone before and with the object of the enactment as stated in its preamble. This Court refused to accept a literal interpretation of the statute, and in effect rectified its language by reading the word "not" into the place where it was evidently intended to go.

The statute before us for interpretation has never been applied literally. Centuries ago it was established that a killing in self-defense is excused. There is nothing in the wording of the statute that suggests this exception. Various attempts have been made to reconcile the legal treatment of self-defense with the words of the statute, but in my opinion these are all merely ingenious sophistries. The truth is that the exception in favor of self-defense cannot be reconciled with the *words* of the statute, but only with its *purpose*.

The true reconciliation of the excuse of self-defense with the statute making it a crime to kill another is to be found in the following line of reasoning. One of the principal objects underlying any criminal legislation is that of deterring men from crime. Now it is apparent that if it were declared to be the law that a killing in self-defense is murder such a rule could not operate in a deterrent manner. A man whose life is threatened will repel his aggressor, whatever the law may say. Looking therefore to the broad purposes of criminal legislation, we may safely declare that this statute was not intended to apply to cases of self-defense.

When the rationale of the excuse of self-defense is thus explained, it becomes apparent that precisely the same reasoning is applicable to the case at bar. If in the future any group of men ever find themselves in the tragic predicament of these defendants, we may be sure that their decision whether to live or die will not be controlled by the contents of our criminal code. Accordingly, if we read this statute intelligently it is apparent that it does not apply to this case. The withdrawal of this situation from the effect of the statute is justified by precisely the same considerations that were applied by our predecessors in office centuries ago to the case of self-defense.

There are those who raise the cry of judicial usurpation whenever a court, after analyzing the purpose of a statute, gives to its words a meaning that is not at once apparent to the casual reader who has not studied the statute closely or examined the objectives it seeks to attain. Let me say emphatically that I accept without reservation the proposition that this Court is bound by the statutes of our Commonwealth and that it exercises its powers in subservience to the duly expressed will of the Chamber of Representatives. The line of reasoning I have applied above raises no question of fidelity to enacted law, though it may possible raise a question of the distinction between intelligent and unintelligent fidelity. No superior wants a servant who lacks the capacity to read between the lines. The stupidest housemaid knows that when she is told "to peel the soup and skim the potatoes" her mistress does not mean what she says. She also knows that when her master tells her to "drop everything and come running" he has overlooked the possibility that she is at the moment in the act of rescuing the baby from the rain barrel. Surely we have a right to expect the same modicum of intelligence from the judiciary. The correction of obvious legislative errors or oversights is not to supplant the legislative will, but to make that will effective.

I therefore conclude that on any aspect under which this case may be viewed these defendants are innocent of the crime of murdering Roger Whetmore, and that the conviction should be set aside.

TATTING, J. In the discharge of my duties as a justice of this Court, I am usually able to dissociate the emotional and intellectual sides of my reactions, and to decide the case before me entirely on the basis of the latter. In passing on this tragic case I find that my usual resources fail me. On the emotional side I find myself torn between sympathy for these men and a feeling of abhorrence and disgust at the monstrous act they committed. I had hoped that I would be able to put these contradictory emotions to one side as irrelevant, and to decide the case on the basis of a convincing and logical demonstration of the result demanded by our law. Unfortunately, this deliverance has not been vouchsafed me.

As I analyze the opinion just rendered by my brother Foster, I find that it is shot through with contradictions and fallacies. Let us begin with this first proposition: these men were not subject to our law because they were not in a "state of civil society" but in a "state of nature." I am not clear why this is so, whether it is because of the thickness of the rock that imprisoned them, or because they were hungry, or because they had set up a "new charter of government" by which the usual rules of law were to be supplanted by a throw of the dice. Other difficulties intrude themselves. If these men passed from the jurisdictions of our law to that of "the law of nature," at what moment did this occur? Was it when the entrance to the cave was blocked, or when the threat of starvation reached a certain undefined degree of intensity, or when the agreement for the throwing of the dice was made? These uncertainties in the doctrine proposed by my brother are capable of producing real difficulties. Suppose, for example, one of these men had had his twenty-first birthday while he was imprisoned within the mountain. On what date would we have to consider that he had attained his majority—when he reached the age of twenty-one, at which time he was, by hypothesis, removed from the effects of our law, or only when he was released from the cave and became again subject to what my brother calls our "positive law"? These difficulties may seem fanciful, yet they only serve to reveal the fanciful nature of the doctrine that is capable of giving rise to them.

But it is not necessary to explore these niceties further to demonstrate the absurdity of my brother's position. Mr. Justice Foster and I are the appointed judges of a court of the Commonwealth of Newgarth, sworn and empowered to administer the laws of that Commonwealth. By what authority do we resolve ourselves into a Court of Nature? If these men were indeed under the law of nature, whence comes our authority to expound and apply the law? Certainly *we* are not in a state of nature.

Let us look at the contents of this code of nature that my brother proposes we adopt as our own and apply to this case. What a topsy-turvy and odious code it is! It is a code in which the law of contracts is more fundamental than the law of murder. It is a code under which a man may make a valid agreement empowering his fellows to eat his own body. Under the provisions of this code, furthermore, such an agreement once made is irrevocable, and if one of the parties attempts to withdraw, the others may take the law into their own hands and enforce the contract by violence—for though my brother passes over in convenient silence the effect of Whetmore's withdrawal, this is the necessary implication of his argument.

The principles my brother expounds contain other implications that cannot be tolerated. He argues that when the defendants set upon Whetmore and killed him (we know not how, perhaps by pounding him with stones) they were only exercising the rights conferred upon them by their bargain. Suppose, however, that Whetmore had had concealed upon his person a revolver, and that when he saw the defendants about to slaughter him he had shot them to death in order to save his own life. My brother's reasoning applied to these facts would make Whetmore out to be a murderer, since the excuse of self-defense would have to be denied to him. If his assailants were acting rightfully in seeking to bring about his death, then of course he could no more plead the excuse that he was defending his own life than could a condemned prisoner who struck down the executioner lawfully attempting to place the noose about his neck.

All of these considerations make it impossible for me to accept the first part of my brother's argument. I can neither accept his notion that these men were under a code of nature which this Court was bound to apply to them, nor can I accept the odious and perverted rules that he would read into that code. I come now to the second part of my brother's opinion, in which he seeks to show that the defendants did not violate the provisions of N.C.S.A. (N.S.) § 12-A.

Here the way, instead of being clear, becomes for me misty and ambiguous, though my brother seems unaware of the difficulties that inhere in his demonstrations.

The gist of my brother's argument may be stated in the following terms: No statute, whatever its language, should be applied in a way that contradicts its purpose. One of the purposes of any criminal statute is to deter. The application of the statute making it a crime to kill another to the peculiar facts of this case would contradict this purpose, for it is impossible to believe that the contents of the criminal code could operate in a deterrent manner on men faced with the alternative of life or death. The reasoning by which this exception is read into the statute is, my brother observes, the same as that which is applied in order to provide the excuse of self-defense.

On the fact of things this demonstration seems very convincing indeed. My brother's interpretation of the rationale of the excuse of self-defense is in fact supported by a decision of this court, *Commonwealth v. Parry,* a precedent I happened to encounter in my research on this case. Though *Commonwealth v. Parry* seems generally to have been overlooked in the texts and subsequent decisions, it supports unambiguously the interpretation my brother has put upon the excuse of self-defense.

Now let me outline briefly, however, the perplexities that assail me when I examine my brother's demonstration more closely. It is true that a statute should be applied in the light of its purpose, and that *one* of the purposes of criminal legislation is recognized to be deterrence. The difficulty is that other purposes are also ascribed to the law of crimes. It has been said that one of its objects is to provide an orderly outlet for the instinctive human demand for retribution. *Commonwealth v. Scape.* It has also been said that its object is the rehabilitation of the wrongdoer. *Commonwealth v. Makeover.* Other theories have been propounded. Assuming that we must interpret a statute in the light of its purpose, what are we to do when it has many purposes or when its purposes are disputed?

A similar difficulty is presented by the fact that although there is authority for my brother's interpretation of the excuse of self-defense, there is other authority which assigns to that excuse a different rationale. Indeed, until I happened on *Commonwealth v.*

Parry I had never heard of the explanation given by my brother. The taught doctrine of our law schools, memorized by generations of law students, runs in the following terms: The statute concerning murder requires a "willful" act. The man who acts to repel an aggressive threat to his own life does not act "willfully," but in response to an impulse deeply ingrained in human nature. I suspect that there is hardly a lawyer in this Commonwealth who is not familiar with this line of reasoning, especially since the point is a great favorite of the bar examiners.

Now the familiar explanation for the excuse of self-defense just expounded obviously cannot be applied by analogy to the facts of this case. These men acted not only "willfully" but with great deliberation and after hours of discussing what they should do. Again we encounter a forked path, with one line of reasoning leading us in one direction and another in a direction that is exactly the opposite. This perplexity is in this case compounded, as it were, for we have to set off one explanation, incorporated in a virtually unknown precedent of this Court, against another explanation, which forms a part of the taught legal tradition of our law schools, but which, so far as I know, has never been adopted in any judicial decision.

I recognize the relevance of the precedents cited by my brother concerning the displaced "not" and the defendant who parked overtime. But what are we to do with one of the landmarks of our jurisprudence, which again my brother passes over in silence? This is *Commonwealth v. Valjean.* Though the case is somewhat obscurely reported, it appears that the defendant was indicted for the larceny of a loaf of bread, and offered as a defense that he was in a condition approaching starvation. The court refused to accept this defense. If hunger cannot justify the theft of wholesome and natural food, how can it justify the killing and eating of a man? Again, if we look at the thing in terms of deterrence, is it likely that a man will starve to death to avoid a jail sentence for the theft of a loaf of bread? My brother's demonstrations would compel us to overrule *Commonwealth v. Valjean,* and many other precedents that have been built on that case.

Again, I have difficulty in saying that no deterrent effect whatever could be attributed to a decision that these men were guilty of murder. The stigma of the word "murderer" is such that it is quite likely, I believe, that if these men had known that their act was deemed by the law to be murder they would have waited for a few days at least before carrying out their plan. During that time some unexpected relief might have come. I realize that this observation only reduces the distinction to a matter of degree, and does not destroy it altogether. It is certainly true that the element of deterrence would be less in this case than is normally involved in the application of the criminal law.

There is still a further difficulty in my brother Foster's proposal to read an exception into the statute to favor this case, though again a difficulty not even intimated in his opinion. What shall be the scope of this exception? Here the men cast lots and the victim was himself originally a party to the agreement. What would we have to decide if Whetmore had refused from the beginning to participate in the plan? Would a majority be permitted to overrule him? Or, suppose that no plan were adopted at all and the others simply conspired to bring about Whetmore's death, justifying their act by saying that he was in the weakest condition. Or again, that a plan of selection was followed but one based on a different justification than the one adopted here, as if the others were atheists and insisted that Whetmore should die because he was the only one who believed in an afterlife. These illustrations could be multiplied, but enough have been suggested to reveal what a quagmire of hidden difficulties my brother's reasoning contains.

Of course I realize on reflection that I may be concerning myself with a problem that will never arise, since it is unlikely that any group of men will ever again be brought to commit the dread act that was involved here. Yet, on still further reflection, even if we are certain that no similar case will arise again, do not the illustrations I have given show the lack of any coherent and rational principle in the rule my brother proposes? Should not the soundness of a principle be tested by the conclusions it entails, without reference to the accidents of later litigational history? Still, if this is so, why is it that we of this Court so often discuss the question whether we are likely to have later occasion to apply a principle urged for the solution of the case before us? Is this a situation where a line of reasoning not originally proper has become sanctioned by precedent, so that we are permitted to apply it and may even be under an obligation to do so?

The more I examine this case and think about it, the more deeply I become involved. My mind becomes entangled in the meshes of the very nets I throw out for my own rescue. I find that almost every consideration that bears on the decision of the case is counterbalanced by an opposing consideration leading in the opposite direction. My brother Foster has not furnished to me, nor can I discover for myself, any formula capable of resolving the equivocations that beset me on all sides.

I have given this case the best thought of which I am capable. I have scarcely slept since it was argued before us. When I feel myself inclined to accept the view of my brother Foster, I am repelled by a feeling that his arguments are intellectually unsound and approach mere rationalization. On the other hand, when I incline toward upholding the conviction, I am struck by the absurdity of directing that these men be put to death when their lives have been saved at the cost of the lives of ten heroic workmen. It is to me a matter of regret that the Prosecutor saw fit to ask for an indictment for murder. If we had a provision in our statutes making it a crime to eat human flesh, that would have been a more appropriate charge. If no other charge suited to the facts of this case could be brought against the defendants, it would have been wiser, I think, not to have indicted them at all. Unfortunately, however, the men have been indicted and tried, and we have therefore been drawn into this unfortunate affair.

Since I have been wholly unable to resolve the doubts that beset me about the law of this case, I am with regret announcing a step that is, I believe, unprecedented in the history of this tribunal. I declare my withdrawal from the decision of this case.

KEEN, J. should like to begin by setting to one side two questions which are not before this Court.

The first of these is whether executive clemency should be extended to these defendants if the conviction is affirmed. Under our system of government, that is a question for the Chief Executive, not for us. I therefore disapprove of that passage in the opinion of the Chief Justice in which he in effect gives instructions to the Chief

Executive as to what he should do in this case and suggests that some impropriety will attach if these instructions are not heeded. This is a confusion of governmental functions—a confusion of which the judiciary should be the last to be guilty. I wish to state that if I were the Chief Executive I would go farther in the direction of clemency than the pleas addressed to him propose. I would pardon these men altogether, since I believe that they have already suffered enough to pay for any offense they may have committed. I want it to be understood that this remark is made in my capacity as a private citizen who by the accident of his office happens to have acquired an intimate acquaintance with the facts of this case. In the discharge of my duties as judge, it is neither my function to address directions to the Chief Executive, nor to take into account what he may or may not do, in reaching my own decision, which must be controlled entirely by the law of this Commonwealth.

The second question that I wish to put to one side is that of deciding whether what these men did was "right" or "wrong," "wicked" or "good." That is also a question that is irrelevant to the discharge of my office as a judge sworn to apply, not my conceptions of morality, but the law of the land. In putting this question to one side I think I can also safely dismiss without comment the first and more poetic portion of my brother Foster's opinion. The element of fantasy contained in the arguments developed there has been sufficiently revealed in my brother Tatting's somewhat solemn attempt to take those arguments seriously.

The sole question before us for decision is whether these defendants did, within the meaning of N.C.S.A. (N.S.) § 12-A, willfully take the life of Roger Whetmore. The exact language of the statute is as follows: "Whoever shall willfully take the life of another shall be punished by death." Now I should suppose that any candid observer, content to extract from these words their natural meaning, would concede at once that these defendants did "willfully take the life" of Roger Whetmore.

Whence arise all the difficulties of the case, then, and the necessity for so many pages of discussion about what ought to be so obvious? The difficulties, in whatever tortured form they may present themselves, all trace back to a single source, and that is a failure to distinguish the legal from the moral aspects of this case. To put it bluntly, my brothers do not like the fact that the written law requires the conviction of these defendants. Neither do I, but unlike my brothers I respect the obligations of an office that requires me to put my personal predilections out of my mind when I come to interpret and apply the law of this Commonwealth.

Now, of course, my brother Foster does not admit that he is actuated by a personal dislike of the written law. Instead he develops a familiar line of argument according to which the court may disregard the express language of a statute when something not contained in the statute itself, called its "purpose," can be employed to justify the result the court considers proper. Because this is an old issue between myself and my colleague, I should like, before discussing his particular application of the argument to the facts of this case, to say something about the historical background of this issue and its implications for law and government generally.

There was a time in this Commonwealth when judges did in fact legislate very freely, and all of us know that during that period some of our statutes were rather thoroughly made over by the judiciary. That was a time when the accepted principles of political science did not designate with any certainty the rank and function of the various arms of the state. We all know the tragic issue of that uncertainty in the brief civil war that arose out of the conflict between the judiciary, on the one hand, and the executive and the legislature, on the other. There is no need to recount here the factors that contributed to that unseemly struggle for power, though they included the unrepresentative character of the Chamber, resulting from a division of the country into election districts that no longer accorded with the actual distribution of the population, and the forceful personality and wide popular following of the then Chief Justice. It is enough to observe that those days are behind us, and that in place of the uncertainty that then reigned we now have a clear-cut principle, which is the supremacy of the legislative branch of our government. From that principle flows the obligation of the judiciary to enforce faithfully the written law, and to interpret that law in accordance with its plain meaning without reference to our personal desires or our individual conceptions of justice. I am not concerned with the question whether the principle that forbids the judicial revision of statutes is right or wrong, desirable or undesirable; I observe merely that this principle has become a tacit premise underlying the whole of the legal and governmental order I am sworn to administer.

Yet though the principle of the supremacy of the legislature has been accepted in theory for centuries, such is the tenacity of professional tradition and the force of fixed habits of thought that many of the judiciary have still not accommodated themselves to the restricted role which the new order imposes on them. My brother Foster is one of that group; his way of dealing with statutes is exactly that of a judge living in the 3900's.

We are all familiar with the process by which the judicial reform of disfavored legislative enactments is accomplished. Anyone who has followed the written opinions of Mr. Justice Foster will have had an opportunity to see it at work in every branch of the law. I am personally so familiar with the process that in the event of my brother's incapacity I am sure I could write a satisfactory opinion for him without any prompting whatever, beyond being informed whether he liked the effect of the terms of the statute as applied to the case before him.

The process of judicial reform requires three steps. The first of these is to divine some single "purpose" which the statute serves. This is done although not one statute in a hundred has any such single purpose, and although the objectives of nearly every statute are differently interpreted by the different classes of its sponsors. The second step is to discover that a mythical being called "the legislator," in the pursuit of this imagined "purpose," overlooked something or left some gap or imperfection in his work. Then comes the final and most refreshing part of the task, which is, of course, to fill in the blank thus created. *Quod erat faciendum.*

My brother Foster's penchant for finding holes in statutes reminds one of the story told by an ancient author about the man who ate a pair of shoes. Asked how he liked them, he replied that the part he liked best was the holes. That is the way my brother feels about statutes; the more holes they have in them the better he likes them. In short, he doesn't like statutes.

One could not wish for a better case to illustrate the specious nature of this gap-filling process than the one before us. My brother thinks he knows exactly what was sought when men made murder a crime, and that was something he calls "deterrence." My brother

Tatting has already shown how much is passed over in that interpretation. But I think the trouble goes deeper. I doubt very much whether our statute making murder a crime really has a "purpose" in any ordinary sense of the term. Primarily, such a statute reflects a deeply-felt human conviction that murder is wrong and that something should be done to the man who commits it. If we were forced to be more articulate about the matter, we would probably take refuge in the more sophisticated theories of the criminologists, which, of course, were certainly not in the minds of those who drafted our statute. We might also observe that men will do their own work more effectively and live happier lives if they are protected against the threat of violent assault. Bearing in mind that the victims of murders are often unpleasant people, we might add some suggestion that the matter of disposing of undesirables is not a function suited to private enterprise, but should be a state monopoly. All of which reminds me of the attorney who once argued before us that a statute licensing physicians was a good thing because it would lead to lower life insurance rates by lifting the level of general health. There is such a thing as overexplaining the obvious.

If we do not know the purpose of § 12-A, how can we possibly say there is a "gap" in it? How can we know what its draftsmen thought about the question of killing men in order to eat them? My brother Tatting has revealed an understandable, though perhaps slightly exaggerated revulsion to cannibalism. How do we know that his remote ancestors did not feel the same revulsion to an even higher degree? Anthropologists say that the dread felt for a forbidden act may be increased by the fact that the conditions of a tribe's life create special temptations toward it, as incest is most severely condemned among those whose village relations make it most likely to occur. Certainly the period following the Great Spiral was one that had implicit in it temptations to anthropophagy. Perhaps it was for that very reason that our ancestors expressed their prohibition in so broad and unqualified a form. All of this is conjecture, of course, but it remains abundantly clear that neither I nor my brother Foster knows what the "purpose" of § 12-A is.

Considerations similar to those I have just outlined are also applicable to the exception in favor of self-defense, which plays so large a role in the reasoning of my brothers Foster and Tatting. It is of course true that in *Commonwealth v. Parry* an obiter dictum justified this exception on the assumption that the purpose of criminal legislation is to deter. It may well also be true that generations of law students have been taught that the true explanation of the exception lies in the fact that a man who acts in self-defense does not act "willfully," and that the same students have passed their bar examinations by repeating what their professors told them. These last observations I could dismiss, of course, as irrelevant for the simple reason that professors and bar examiners have not as yet any commission to make our laws for us. But again the real trouble lies deeper. As in dealing with the statute, so in dealing with the exception, the question is not the conjectural *purpose* of the rule, but its *scope*. Now the scope of the exception in favor of self-defense as it has been applied by this Court is plain: it applies to cases of resisting an aggressive threat to the party's own life. It is therefore too clear for argument that this case does not fall within the scope of the exception, since it is plain that Whetmore made no threat against the lives of these defendants.

The essential shabbiness of my brother Foster's attempt to cloak his remaking of the written law with an air of legitimacy comes tragically to the surface in my brother Tatting's opinion. In that opinion Justice Tatting struggles manfully to combine his colleague's loose moralisms with his own sense of fidelity to the written law. The issue of this struggle could only be that which occurred, a complete default in the discharge of the judicial function. You simply cannot apply a statute as it is written and remake it to meet your own wishes at the same time.

Now I know that the line of reasoning I have developed in this opinion will not be acceptable to those who look only to the immediate effects of a decision and ignore the long-run implications of an assumption by the judiciary of a power of dispensation. A hard decision is never a popular decision. Judges have been celebrated in literature for their sly prowess in devising some quibble by which a litigant could be deprived of his rights where the public thought it was wrong for him to assert those rights. But I believe that judicial dispensation does more harm in the long run than hard decisions. Hard cases may even have a certain moral value by bringing home to the people their own responsibilities toward the law that is ultimately their creation, and by reminding them that there is no principle of personal grace that can relieve the mistakes of their representatives.

Indeed, I will go farther and say that not only are the principles I have been expounding those which are soundest for our present conditions, but that we would have inherited a better legal system from our forefathers if those principles had been observed from the beginning. For example, with respect to the excuse of self-defense, if our courts had stood steadfast on the language of the statute the result would undoubtedly have been a legislative revision of it. Such a revision would have drawn on the assistance of natural philosophers and psychologists, and the resulting regulation of the matter would have had an understandable and rational basis, instead of the hodgepodge of verbalisms and metaphysical distinctions that have emerged from the judicial and professorial treatment.

These concluding remarks are, of course, beyond any duties that I have to discharge with relation to this case, but I include them here because I feel deeply that my colleagues are insufficiently aware of the dangers implicit in the conceptions of the judicial office advocated by my brother Foster.

I conclude that the conviction should be affirmed.

HANDY, J. I have listened with amazement to the tortured ratiocinations to which this simple case has given rise. I never cease to wonder at my colleagues' ability to throw an obscuring curtain of legalisms about every issue presented to them for decision. We have heard this afternoon learned disquisitions on the distinction between positive law and the law of nature, the language of the statute and the purpose of the statute, judicial functions and executive functions, judicial legislation and legislative legislation. My only disappointment was that someone did not raise the question of the legal nature of the bargain struck in the cave—whether it was unilateral or bilateral, and whether Whetmore could not be considered as having revoked an offer prior to action taken thereunder.

What have all these things to do with the case? The problem before us is what we, as officers of the government, ought to do with these defendants. That is a question of practical wisdom, to be exercised in a context, not of abstract theory, but of human realities. When the case is approached in this light, it becomes, I think, one of the easiest to decide that has ever been argued before this Court.

Before stating my own conclusions about the merits of the case, I should like to discuss briefly some of the more fundamental issues involved—issues on which my colleagues and I have been divided ever since I have been on the bench.

I have never been able to make my brothers see that government is a human affair, and that men are ruled, not by words on paper or by abstract theories, but by other men. They are ruled well when their rulers understand the feelings and conceptions of the masses. They are ruled badly when that understanding is lacking.

Of all branches of the government, the judiciary is the most likely to lose its contact with the common man. The reasons for this are, of course, fairly obvious. Where the masses react to a situation in terms of a few salient features, we pick into little pieces every situation presented to us. Lawyers are hired by both sides to analyze and dissect. Judges and attorneys vie with one another to see who can discover the greatest number of difficulties and distinctions in a single set of facts. Each side tries to find cases, real or imagined, that will embarrass the demonstrations of the other side. To escape this embarrassment, still further distinctions are invented and imported into the situation. When a set of facts has been subjected to this kind of treatment for a sufficient time, all the life and juice have gone out of it and we have left a handful of dust.

Now I realize that wherever you have rules and abstract principles lawyers are going to be able to make distinctions. To some extent the sort of thing I have been describing is a necessary evil attaching to any formal regulation of human affairs. But I think that the area which really stands in need of such regulation is greatly overestimated. There are, of course, a few fundamental rules of the game that must be accepted if the game is to go on at all. I would include among these the rules relating to the conduct of elections, the appointment of public officials, and the term during which an office is held. Here some restraint on discretion and dispensation, some adherence to form, some scruple for what does and what does not fall within the rule, is, I concede, essential. Perhaps the area of basic principle should be expanded to include certain other rules, such as those designed to preserve the free civilmoign system.

But outside of these fields I believe that all government officials, including judges, will do their jobs best if they treat forms and abstract concepts as instruments. We should take as our model, I think, the good administrator, who accommodates procedures and principles to the case at hand, selecting from among the available forms those most suited to reach the proper result.

The most obvious advantage of this method of government is that it permits us to go about our daily tasks with efficiency and common sense. My adherence to this philosophy has, however, deeper roots. I believe that it is only with the insight this philosophy gives that we can preserve the flexibility essential if we are to keep our actions in reasonable accord with the sentiments of those subject to our rule. More governments have been wrecked, and more human misery caused, by the lack of this accord between ruler and ruled than by any other factor that can be discerned in history. Once drive a sufficient wedge between the mass of people and those who direct their legal, political, and economic life, and our society is ruined. Then neither Foster's law of nature nor Keen's fidelity to written law will avail us anything.

Now when these conceptions are applied to the case before us, its decision becomes, as I have said, perfectly easy. In order to demonstrate this I shall have to introduce certain realities that my brothers in their coy decorum have seen fit to pass over in silence, although they are just as acutely aware of them as I am.

The first of these is that this case has aroused an enormous public interest, both here and abroad. Almost every newspaper and magazine has carried articles about it; columnists have shared with their readers confidential information as to the next governmental move; hundreds of letters-to-the-editor have been printed. One of the great newspaper chains made a poll of public opinion on the question, "What do you think the Supreme Court should do with the Speluncean explorers?" About ninety per cent expressed a belief that the defendants should be pardoned or let off with a kind of token punishment. It is perfectly clear, then, how the public feels about the case. We could have known this without the poll, of course, on the basis of common sense, or even by observing that on this Court there are apparently four-and-a-half men, or ninety per cent, who share the common opinion.

This makes it obvious, not only what we should do, but what we must do if we are to preserve between ourselves and public opinion a reasonable and decent accord. Declaring these men innocent need not involve us in any undignified quibble or trick. No principle of statutory construction is required that is not consistent with the past practices of this Court. Certainly no layman would think that in letting these men off we had stretched the statute any more than our ancestors did when they created the excuse of self-defense. If a more detailed demonstration of the method of reconciling our decision with the statute is required, I should be content to rest on the arguments developed in the second and less visionary part of my brother Foster's opinion.

Now I know that my brothers will be horrified by my suggestion that this Court should take account of public opinion. They will tell you that public opinion is emotional and capricious, that it is based on half-truths and listens to witnesses who are not subject to cross-examination. They will tell you that the law surrounds the trial of a case like this with elaborate safeguards, designed to insure that the truth will be known and that every rational consideration bearing on the issues of the case has been taken into account. They will warn you that all of these safeguards go for naught if a mass opinion formed outside this framework is allowed to have any influence on our decision.

But let us look candidly at some of the realities of the administration of our criminal law. When a man is accused of crime, there are, speaking generally, four ways in which he may escape punishment. One of these is a determination by a judge that under the applicable law he has committed no crime. This is, of course, a determination that takes place in a rather formal and abstract atmosphere. But look at the other three ways in which he may escape punishment. These are: (1) a decision by the Prosecutor not to ask for an indictment; (2) an acquittal by the jury; (3) a pardon or commutation of sentence by the executive. Can anyone pretend that these decisions are held within a rigid and formal framework of rules that prevents factual error, excludes emotional and personal factors, and guarantees that all the forms of the law will be observed?

In the case of the jury we do, to be sure, attempt to cabin their deliberations within the area of the legally relevant, but there is no need to deceive ourselves into believing that this attempt is really successful. In the normal course of events the case now before us would have gone on all of its issues directly to the jury. Had this occurred we can be confident that there would have been an acquittal or at least a division that would have prevented a conviction. If the jury had been instructed that the men's hunger and their agreement were no defense to the charge of murder, their verdict would in all likelihood have ignored this instruction and would have involved a good deal more twisting of the letter of the law than any that is likely to tempt us. Of course the only reason that didn't occur in this case was the fortuitous circumstance that the foreman of the jury happened to be a lawyer. His learning enabled him to devise a form of words that would allow the jury to dodge its usual responsibilities.

My brother Tatting expresses annoyance that the Prosecutor did not, in effect, decide the case for him by not asking for an indictment. Strict as he is himself in complying with the demands of legal theory, he is quite content to have the fate of these men decided out of court by the Prosecutor on the basis of common sense. The Chief Justice, on the other hand, wants the application of common sense postponed to the very end, though like Tatting, he wants no personal part in it.

This brings me to the concluding portion of my remarks, which has to do with executive clemency. Before discussing that topic directly, I want to make a related observation about the poll of public opinion. As I have said, ninety per cent of the people wanted the Supreme Court to let the men off entirely or with a more or less nominal punishment. The ten per cent constituted a very oddly assorted group, with the most curious and divergent opinions. One of our university experts has made a study of this group and has found that its members fall into certain patterns. A substantial portion of them are subscribers to "crank" newspapers of limited circulation that gave their readers a distorted version of the facts of the case. Some thought that "Speluncean" means "cannibal" and that anthropophagy is a tenet of the Society. But the point I want to make, however, is this: although almost every conceivable variety and shade of opinion was represented in this group, there was, so far as I know, not one of them, nor a single member of the majority of ninety per cent, who said, "I think it would be a fine thing to have the courts sentence these men to be hanged, and then to have another branch of the government come along and pardon them." Yet this is a solution that has more or less dominated our discussions and which our Chief Justice proposes as a way by which we can avoid doing an injustice and at the same time preserve respect for law. He can be assured that if he is preserving anybody's morale, it is his own, and not the public's, which knows nothing of his distinctions. I mention this matter because I wish to emphasize once more the danger that we may get lost in the patterns of our own thought and forget that these patterns often cast not the slightest shadow on the outside world.

I come now to the most crucial facts in this case, a fact known to all of us on this Court, though one that my brothers have seen fit to keep under the cover of their judicial robes. This is the frightening likelihood that if the issue is left to him, the Chief Executive will refuse to pardon these men or commute their sentence. As we all know, our Chief Executive is a man now well advanced in years, of very stiff notions. Public clamor usually operates on him with the reverse of the effect intended. As I have told my brothers, it happens that my wife's niece is an intimate friend of his secretary. I have learned in this indirect, but, I think, wholly reliable way, that he is firmly determined not to commute the sentence if these men are found to have violated the law.

No one regrets more than I the necessity for relying in so important a matter on information that could be characterized as gossip. If I had my way this would not happen, for I would adopt the sensible course of sitting down with the Executive, going over the case with him, finding out what his views are, and perhaps working out with him a common program for handling the situation. But of course my brothers would never hear of such a thing.

Their scruple about acquiring accurate information directly does not prevent them from being very perturbed about what they have learned indirectly. Their acquaintance with the facts I have just related explains why the Chief Justice, ordinarily a model of decorum, saw fit in his opinion to flap his judicial robes in the face of the Executive and threaten him with excommunication if he failed to commute the sentence. It explains, I suspect, my brother Foster's feat of levitation by which a whole library of law books was lifted from the shoulders of these defendants. It explains also why even my legalistic brother Keen emulated Pooh-Bah in the ancient comedy by stepping to the other side of the stage to address a few remarks to the Executive "in my capacity as a private citizen." (I may remark, incidentally, that the advice of Private Citizen Keen will appear in the reports of this court printed at taxpayers' expense.)

I must confess that as I grow older I become more and more perplexed at men's refusal to apply their common sense to problems of law and government, and this truly tragic case has deepened my sense of discouragement and dismay. I only wish that I could convince my brothers of the wisdom of the principles I have applied to the judicial office since I first assumed it. As a matter of fact, by a kind of sad rounding of the circle, I encountered issues like those involved here in the very first case I tried as Judge of the Court of General Instances in Fanleigh County.

A religious sect had unfrocked a minister who, they said, had gone over to the views and practices of a rival sect. The minister circulated a handbill making charges against the authorities who had expelled him. Certain lay members of the church announced a public meeting at which they proposed to explain the position of the church. The minister attended this meeting. Some said he slipped in unobserved in a disguise; his own testimony was that he had walked in openly as a member of the public. At any rate, when the speeches began he interrupted with certain questions about the affairs of the church and made some statements in defense of his own views. He was set upon by members of the audience and given a pretty thorough pommeling, receiving among other injuries a broken jaw. He brought a suit for damages against the association that sponsored the meeting and against ten named individuals who he alleged were his assailants.

When we came to the trial, the case at first seemed very complicated to me. The attorneys raised a host of legal issues. There were nice questions on the admissibility of evidence, and, in connection with the suit against the association, some difficult problems turning on the question whether the minister was a trespasser or a licensee. As a novice on the bench I was eager to apply my law school learning and I began studying these questions closely, reading all the authorities and preparing well-documented rulings. As I studied the case I became more and more involved in its legal intricacies and I began to get into a state approaching that of my brother Tatting in this case. Suddenly, however, it dawned on me that all these perplexing issues really had nothing to do with the case, and I began examining it in the light of common sense. The case at once gained a new perspective, and I saw that the only thing for me to do was to direct a verdict for the defendants for lack of evidence.

I was led to this conclusion by the following considerations. The melee in which the plaintiff was injured had been a very confused affair, with some people trying to get to the center of the disturbance, while others were trying to get away from it; some striking at the plaintiff, while others were apparently trying to protect him. It would have taken weeks to find out the truth of the matter. I decided that nobody's broken jaw was worth that much to the Commonwealth. (The minister's injuries, incidentally, had meanwhile healed without disfigurement and without any impairment of normal faculties.) Furthermore, I felt very strongly that the plaintiff had to a large extent brought the thing on himself. He knew how inflamed passions were about the affair, and could easily have found another forum for the expression of his views. My decision was widely approved by the press and public opinion, neither of which could tolerate the views and practices that the expelled minister was attempting to defend.

Now, thirty years later, thanks to an ambitious Prosecutor and a legalistic jury foreman, I am faced with a case that raises issues which are at bottom much like those involved in that case. The world does not seem to change much, except that this time it is not a question of a judgment for five or six hundred frelars, but of the life or death of four men who have already suffered more torment and humiliation than most of us would endure in a thousand years. I conclude that the defendants are innocent of the crime charged, and that the conviction and sentence should be set aside.

TATTING, J. I have been asked by the Chief Justice whether, after listening to the two opinions just rendered, I desire to reexamine the position previously taken by me. I wish to state that after hearing these opinions I am greatly strengthened in my conviction that I ought not to participate in the decision of this case.

The Supreme Court being evenly divided, the conviction and sentence of the Court of General Instances is *affirmed.* It is ordered that the execution of the sentence shall occur at 6 A.M., Friday, April 2, 4300, at which time the Public Executioner is directed to proceed with all convenient dispatch to hang each of the defendants by the neck until he is dead.

CHAPTER 6. THE SPELUNCEAN EXPLORERS—FURTHER PROCEEDINGS

Now that you've read the Great Case, and while your mind is full of questions about it, here is a sequel that I wrote a few years ago. Unfortunately for me, Professor Fuller did not live to see it. If he had, I'm sure I would have received from him a wonderfully marked up copy, full of thoughts and comments and criticisms. (He did precisely that with a book I published in 1971 on the concept of custom, and his estate was kind enough to give his copy of the book to me. Professor Fuller's thoroughly annotated running commentary of my book is the most treasured item in my library.)

ADVISORY OPINIONS OF THE SPECIAL COMMISSION

The Chief Executive of Newgarth has constituted this Special Commission to present its report and recommendations on the question whether executive clemency should be extended to the four defendants in the notorious "Case of the Speluncean Explorers." Their conviction for murder was upheld on March 20, 4300, by the Supreme Court in a divided opinion.

The Special Commission consists of three professors of law at the University of Newgarth School of Law. Since after intense deliberation the Commission has been unable to present a single consensus report, our findings will consist of this general introductory statement which has been subscribed to by all three members of the Commission, followed by the individual recommendation of each member. We have each concluded that our own opinion is correct and the other two are flatly wrong. Our shared commitment to the rule of law precludes us from voting or otherwise combining our opinions, because we believe that the weight of numbers is ultimately a matter of power and not of right or reason. Thus we find ourselves in the position of only being able to endorse these preliminary remarks and otherwise insisting upon the logic of our own separate opinions. Each of us hopes that his or her own opinion will be persuasive to the Chief Executive in his difficult task of deciding whether to exercise his right of executive clemency.

Our individual differences may be great, but we share a total commitment to what Professor Fuller called "fidelity to law." The oral tradition of his teachings has gained in persuasive force through the centuries even though his writings were of course destroyed in the holocaust following the Great Spiral. Unfortunately, his insistence that fidelity to law is a matter of morality—the morality of aspiration—does not seem to have been accepted by at least two justices of our Supreme Court. Justice Handy's theory, that a case ought to be decided in the unchecked discretion of the judges according to what is administratively convenient, is antithetical to the possibility of the rule of law. And Justice Tatting's inability to reach a decision in the case involves a denial that the law can be knowable before a judge is called upon to apply it.

On these preliminary remarks we all agree. We now proceed to attach to this report our separate opinions addressed to the Chief Executive.

Opinion of Professor Wun

When I received news of the decision in this case, I was relieved that the Court had reached the only proper result. But later, as I read the opinion of the justices, I realized how fragile the Court's decision really was. To recap the vote, Justices Handy and Foster voted for acquittal, Tatting withdrew from the case, and although Keen and Truepenny voted to affirm the finding of guilty they engaged in powerful pleas to the Chief Executive to extend clemency to the convicted defendants. Not one of them came even close to believing, as I do, that the defendants were clearly guilty of murder. Perhaps the most egregiously bankrupt opinion illustrating the Court's true feeling is that of Justice Keen, who found it necessary to resort to the old and discredited theory of positivism to prop up his conclusion. He insisted upon a separation between law and morality, holding that "the law" required a finding of guilty even though his own morality would lead to a different result. Without repeating familiar arguments against this positivistic stance, it may suffice to ask what morality compels Justice Keen to insist upon a separation between law and morality.

Since I believe that matters of right cannot be separated from matters of law, I might most efficiently begin by showing that what these defendants did is murder as a matter of morality, and only after that turn to the legal conclusion that murder was committed. As moral arguments are often best proved by analogies, let us consider four persons on the brink of death due to, respectively, a defective heart, diseased lungs, a destroyed liver, and a non-functioning kidney. Since their lives are at stake their "need" to have these organs replaced by healthy ones could not possibly be greater. We will assume that there are no replacement organs available. The four persons thereupon decide that they will kidnap a stranger who is in good health, take him to a medical office where they have several highly paid doctors waiting, kill the stranger, and have the doctors transplant his four healthy organs into the four conspirators. Four lives will thus be saved at the cost of only one, and the result can be said to have been objectively compelled by "necessity" and not by any personal malice toward the stranger or any wish to harm him.

I will assume that anyone would immediately conclude that these four persons would be morally guilty of murdering the stranger (and, consequently, that they should be prosecuted under the law for murder). But then, of course, we must ask whether there is any significant difference between the hypothetical and the speluncean explorers. Certainly not because the victim was a stranger whereas Whetmore was known to the explorers. For the case would not be morally improved if the four persons needing organ transplants had instead selected a victim who had been friendly with them. But, one might object, Whetmore was involved in the same enterprise as the other explorers; that surely makes a difference. Yet consider the following alteration: The four persons, partners in a research team, had their vital organs damaged because their machine had broken and emitted omicron rays. A fifth co-worker was also present, but miraculously she was not hurt. Are the four damaged individuals thereby entitled to kill her and transplant her organs simply because she was involved in the same enterprise and at the same time as they?

What of another possible distinction: that Whetmore was going to die shortly of malnutrition anyway, whereas the stranger in the hypothetical case was in good health? Does that fact give the explorers a moral right to kill Whetmore? What if the persons needing transplants read in the papers that doctors had informed a certain individual that he had only six more months left to live? Would they be justified in kidnapping and killing that individual because his interest in living only six months is negligible in comparison with the four of them surviving for many years if they can have his organs? But even the six months can be questioned. The doctors might have been in error as to his good health; or the doctors may have been correct but a month later a cure could be discovered. Possibilities always exist, and they existed even for Whetmore. For the explorers trapped in the cave could not be certain that they would not be rescued the next day or even the next hour. Suppose the engineers had been wrong or that another entrance to the cave had been found and the defendants had been rescued two hours after they had killed and eaten Whetmore; would the justices of our Supreme Court have been as sympathetic about the murder?

Let us look more deeply at estimating the possibility of survival for the four defendants trapped in the cave and the four persons needing organ transplants in the hypothetical case. Surely we cannot coerce them to be optimistic about the chance of rescue or of some dramatic medical breakthrough. They have the right to assess the odds for themselves. My contention is simply that they cannot force their version of the odds for survival upon Whetmore or upon the individual who was told he had six months to live.

But such a conclusion does not mean that we should give them a privilege of acting "out of necessity" to harm or kill someone else. At the very most they might decide upon a procedure to save most of their own lives at the expense of one or more of their own number. For example, since each of the four persons needing transplants needed a different organ, any three of them could survive with the healthy organs of the fourth. Suppose the four of them are in the medical office and they put on the table four identical-looking pills, three of which are placebos and the fourth an instantaneous deadly poison. If each selects a pill one would die and his or her organs could immediately be transplanted to the others. Such a procedure, incidentally, would not involve any of them actually killing any of the others; at worst they would each be guilty of attempted suicide and the victim would be guilty of actual suicide. But from a moral point of view, I tend to believe at the present time—unless someone persuades me that I have not refined my personal code of morality sufficiently and that further thought would lead to a different conclusion—that the four persons had a moral right to decide that three survivors would be better than no survivors and that such a procedure would thus be justifiable. Note that the decision to go ahead with the pill-taking was the result of the informed consent of all four persons, each of whom arrived independently at the conclusion that the odds of survival if no action was taken were negligible. The willingness to go ahead with this desperate procedure would prove the genuineness of each individual's decision as to the odds of survival.

Let us apply analogous reasoning to the explorers. Roger Whetmore, for his own reasons, which may have included optimism in a greater degree than any of the other explorers about the chances of an early rescue, did not want to participate in the cannibalism scheme. To be sure there are complicating elements: Whetmore first proposed such a scheme, he carried the dice used to cast lots, and he initially agreed to participate. Yet surely none of these points either in themselves or when taken together estops Whetmore to withdraw, or sets up some sort of reliance by the others such that Whetmore could not fairly withdraw from the scheme. Their charging him with a "breach of faith" is outrageous. Such a charge might properly be levelled at one who attempted to withdraw from the scheme after being designated the victim, but it cannot be applied to a person who withdrew prior to the throw. Although the Justices of our Supreme Court have glossed over the significance of Whetmore's withdrawal, to me the point is of critical importance. By withdrawing, Whetmore both avoided the risk of being killed by the others and denied himself the chance to survive if the others went ahead with their plan. He chose to risk nothing and had nothing to gain. Certainly such an action cannot be labelled as unfair to others.

The others, however, *did have something to gain* by including Whetmore. To be sure, by including Whetmore, the others were taking a risk that Whetmore might end a winner. Curiously, however, when we examine the odds involved, the fact that Whetmore could be a winner is not as significant as the fact that he could be the loser. Consider the four men only. If one of them is to die so that the others will be saved, then each man's chance of dying is one in four, or 25%. If we include Whetmore, each man's chance of dying now becomes one in five, or 20%. In short, each of the four defendants in this case calculated—and they certainly did so calculate, for we know from the testimony that there was much discussion of the mathematical problems involved—that his own chance of survival *increased* by five percentage points from 75% to 80% if Whetmore was included. The forcible inclusion of Whetmore was distinctly in their self-interest. The motive for murder is clear.

Additionally we should not lose sight of the fact that the others had to *kill* Whetmore. A suicide procedure analogous to the pill-taking hypothetical might have been preferable in itself, but *such a procedure was not available to them.* We know Whetmore refused to throw the dice. Clearly he would have refused to take a pill. By his refusal to participate, Whetmore placed the burden of action upon the others. They had to kill him. In fact, they murdered him.

Although I believe that the preceding arguments establish the defendants' moral guilt, I recognize the possible objection that my position against the "necessity" excuse in criminal law proves too much. Surely there are situations where necessity is a legitimate excuse. What if Whetmore discovered on the twentieth day that his pickaxes which he purchased with his own money, had a hollow handle filled with condensed food pills to be used in case of emergency. Assume that there are enough pills so that Whetmore and his companions could survive for another two weeks. Assume further that Whetmore had come to loathe his companions and offers only to sell them food pills at astronomical prices. When his companions accept his price, Whetmore decides that they could not be trusted to pay once they are freed from the cave, and so he asks for immediate payment in cash. At this point, would his companions have the moral right to take some of the pills away from Whetmore by force? I would say yes. But the distinguishing feature of this hypothetical is that a *property right* is being sacrificed to save one or more lives, whereas in the real case, we are considering that a *life* can be sacrificed to save other lives. In short, property-for-life involves rights on a different level whereas life-for-life involves rights on the same level. And when we operate on the same level, necessity is not a justification. Even in a property-for-property case, for example, a man facing bankruptcy cannot justifiably steal money from someone else so that he can save his own property.

At first blush my analysis may appear to be challenged by *Commonwealth v. Valjean*, a case cited by Justice Tatting, which refused to accept the excuse that the defendant stole a loaf of bread because he was starving. I suppose the court paused seriously over the trade between property and life in that case, but must have decided as it did because a decision in the defendant's favor would have had enormously disruptive consequences for society. For if the law were to allow the theft of property by a starving man, many people might soon put themselves into a condition approaching starvation (for example, by first squandering their money in a gambling parlor) and then use that condition as an excuse for stealing food or money without restraint. Thus the harshness of the result to the defendant in *Valjean* is dictated by the need to deter others from exploiting such an "excuse." In contrast, the facts of the speluncean explorers clearly preclude the possibility of general exploitation for the purpose of obtaining nutriment.

Suppose we alter my hypothetical so that Whetmore finds enough pills only to keep one person alive for two weeks. Then if the others force him to share the pills, each will be kept alive for two or three days, but not until the rescue team breaks in ten days later. In that case, Whetmore would be justified in keeping all the pills for himself. But then this is not a case of property winning over lives, it is still a life-for-life case. For if the others forcibly took away from Whetmore the pills he needed to survive, they would be killing him, even though they may have then redistributed to Whetmore a two- or three-day supply equal to each of theirs. Thus even the *Valjean* case, upon further reflection, may be seen as a life-for-life case and thus explainable as directly analogous to the real case of the speluncean explorers. For if hungry people could steal loaves of bread, farmers would not grow as much wheat and bakers would not make loaves of bread for sale to others. The shortage of food would mean that all would starve, including the farmer, since starving men would take away all of his wheat. Allowing theft not only destroys the incentive to produce in order to sell to others, but also destroys the ability to grow wheat for one's own consumption, since as soon as it is grown it will be stolen by hordes of starving people. In brief, it may be very hard to find a true "necessity" case. And if my first pickaxe hypothetical example is such a case, it is different from that of the speluncean explorers.

Let us turn now to the legal analysis, which is coincident with the moral argument previously given. Clearly the statute under which the defendants were convicted covers the present case. Section 12-A of the Consolidated Statutes of Newgarth, N.C.S.A. (N.S.) § 12-A, provides: "Whoever shall willfully take the life of another shall be punished by death." I do not have to explore the question whether this statute admits of exceptions, and I need not repeat the arguments of the Justices of our Supreme Court on the question of whether self-defense is one such exception. Suffice it to say that if the statute does allow for exceptions, "necessity" is not one of them since it is a life-for-life and not a property-for-life case.

Nor am I troubled by Justice Foster's argument that the explorers, trapped in the cave, were removed from the jurisdiction of Newgarth and hence the law cannot be applied to them. For one thing, the explorers are nationals and citizens of Newgarth, and on that basis our criminal laws may be extended to them even if they were outside the territorial limits of Newgarth. (Of course they were not; they were in a cave within the Commonwealth.) Second, they killed a national of Newgarth and thereby harmed the Commonwealth itself; accordingly Newgarth has a right of vindication through its criminal law process. Third, the defendants expected to be rescued by citizens of Newgarth, and hence their "captors"—the first persons who would have jurisdiction over them—would be persons subject to our laws. Fourth, the taking of the life of another is the gravest possible violation of a human right enjoyed by everyone wherever located. Even if Judge Foster were correct that legislative power did not reach these explorers in their cave, our laws would provide a statutory and administrative basis for enforcing the universal prohibition against murder wherever perpetrated.

Finally, legal analysis requires us to consider the purpose of the statute. The purpose of the present or any other criminal statute is not primarily to punish someone for a past act, but to deter the act from ever taking place. Such statutes institutionalize rights—the rights accorded to every person to not be the victim of criminal acts. The purpose of the statute in the present case, therefore, is to give to potential murder victims the protective power of the state. We might imagine Roger Whetmore saying something like the following to the four explorers as they advanced upon him: "What you are about to do is to commit murder. If you do so, and you survive and are rescued from this cave, the Commonwealth of Newgarth will try, convict, and execute you for murder. So do not attempt to kill me. I have not participated in your casting of lots, and you have no rights against me. Either try to hold out a while longer, as I have decided to do, or else do whatever you feel you must among the four of you alone. But do not include me; the law protects me against death at your hands."

Some such statement, I submit, is the only protection that the Whetmores of this Commonwealth may have when they are outnumbered and cannot protect themselves. As I have said earlier, the situation need not be so rare as explorers trapped in a cave; it includes my organ-transplant hypothetical, and any situation where a potential victim must rely on the law for protection. Our Supreme Court has upheld the law. Certainly as Chief Executive you should not undercut the sanction provided by the statute by commuting the sentence. What the defendants did in this case they did willfully. They acted out of self-interest, to increase the odds of their individual survival by forcibly including Whetmore. Now each defendant should pay fully for the murder he committed to advance his self-interest at the expense of the life of another.

Opinion of Professor Tieu

As my colleague Professor Wun knows, I have always found it difficult to accept any conclusion he reaches. The present case is the clearest example so far. I believe that the four defendants are innocent of any crime. Since I disagree with Professor Wun's conclusion but not his logic, the difficulty must lie in his premises.

His position rests upon a common, unstated, and usually unchallenged assumption that we are all discrete individuals and that the laws of murder provide an essentially nonrational zero-sum game rule for individual players competing with each other. I disagree with his implied definition of human life.

At the most fundamental level, the possibility of human life on earth rests upon the fate of the group, not the individual. The truism that "man is a social animal" tends to hide under a mask of triviality the ultimate fact that for the human species to survive, the individual must be subordinated to the welfare of the group. If, for example, a terrible disease destroyed all but a thousand members of the human race, and left only a hundred of these capable of reproduction, nothing would be more immoral than to sacrifice these fertile survivors before the others.

Because people have minds of their own, they tend to think that their own welfare has supreme value. Yet the desire for group preservation, over and above individual preservation, has stronger roots. To fully appreciate this point, we might profitably consider two kinds of behavior observed in other species: the warning behavior and the leadership phenomenon.

An impala will warn the rest of the herd if it spots a nearby lion; the repeated warning snorts enable the herd to run away, but the warner risks its life. A gazelle warns its fellows by leaping repeatedly stifflegged on all four feet. Yet this permits an approaching pack of predatory dogs to catch up with the gazelle that gives warning even though the rest of the herd escapes. What is noteworthy about these and other instances that have been reported of the "warning" function is that, under standard evolutionary theory, the warners should have been "selected out" eons ago. Clearly what is happening is that the group is being saved by an hereditary characteristic that causes the death of some of the members of the group. Species survival exceeds the survival of individuals, and it is not extinguished even though the individuals who give the warning are sacrificed.

As a further behavioral example, within a given territory or grouping of like animals, a particular animal is deferred to as the leader of the group. The leader is easy to identify; it is usually given the best food, choice of mate or mates, and the other animals respond to its movements as if they are commands. Should the leader be killed, the group will find an individual animal—who previously had only been a follower—to inherit the leadership mantle and assume that position. From an evolutionary point of view, the problem here is not the extinction of the leadership characteristic (as it was in the case of warners), but rather why the leadership trait has not become dominant. The leader of the group typically has the most offspring (due to choice of mates and other perquisites of leadership) and yet, over the centuries, the group's "follower" characteristic has not been extinguished. The answer, again, must be that leading and following are not individual characteristics but rather are functions of the group.

The "warning" and "leadership" behaviors have always been a part of human society. We have many words that indicate behaviors similar to the sacrificial warning behavior of animals: courage, heroism, martyrdom, nobility, gallantry, altruism, and so forth. When a group of people—or a nation—is endangered, these traits blossom forth in some individuals so that the group may be protected. Yet self-sacrifice is not selected out; courage and heroism never die. Similarly, leadership—not only political but also in the arts and sciences and in social groupings—is a commonplace event. We are in fact so accustomed to these behaviors that their importance has to be stressed here.

One could object at this point that I have only *described* behavior in some animals and some humans that points to the paramountcy of group survival, and that we cannot derive from this description a normative statement that would govern how all humans *ought* to behave. In other words, an "is" cannot produce an "ought." My reply is twofold. First, I deny that an "ought" does not follow from an "is." Our entire normative mode of reasoning rests upon our conviction that some things, as a consequence of their existence, should be maintained. For example, our life-supporting environment is a fact; from it we derive the proposition that we have a duty to maintain the environment not only for all humans in existence but for future generations as well. The very notion of a normative principle can have no meaning if it excludes the most fundamental imperative of all: that since human life exists, it ought to be maintained. If we cannot *ought* to continue to exist, then, I submit, we do not really know what is valuable, and without this, we cannot know the meaning of the term "ought" at all. In my previous examples, we saw that a group of animals could owe its continued existence to the genetic trait manifested in some of them who, at sacrificial cost, warned the rest of imminent danger. The only one who could conclude that the warning behavior was valueless would be one who denies that there is any value whatsoever in living. Such a person could not give any meaning to the term "morality," much less comment on whether morality can be derived from fact. Those who understand what "morality" means ultimately trace their understanding to observations of fact. Second, even if I must assume for the moment that "ought" cannot be derived from "is," my previous examples reduce to highly suggestive claims. Anyone looking dispassionately at the warning behavior in a social grouping of animals would have to concede that nature is trying to tell us something! And what nature is saying, rather unambiguously, is that "life" consists of the continued existence of the group rather than any of its members.

So far I have been somewhat abstract in defining the "life" of a group, and the definition should be made precise. Each particular animal is the manifestation of the blueprints of its genes, and is the carrier of those genes. Bodies are in reality only the temporary supporters of the genes. The living genes are truly immortal, so long as the species which supports them continues to survive.

From this last observation I derive the ultimate moral imperative: that one may not destroy the possibility of reproduction. I think we have always perceived this fact even though it tends to go unnoticed in the routine of our lives. What are our laws but expressions of concern for group survival? From the lowliest traffic ordinance to the prohibition against genocide, the laws bespeak social preservation. If the perceptions of how society is best preserved change, the laws will surely change as well—even law which seems clear and unchangeable. As an example, we might briefly reflect upon the history of abortion.

In the period following the Great Spiral, there was a perceived fear that human life might be snuffed out completely. Our numbers were small and the conditions of living were harsh. At that time a human fetus was considered a "life in being" and hence abortion was universally condemned as "murder" under the laws. But after several centuries of population growth and normal conditions, the laws against abortion were honored more in the breach than in the observance. Although religions continued to consider abortion a grave sin, hardly anyone was criminally prosecuted. Finally, in the modern era, overpopulation, and not underpopulation, is considered a grave threat to human survival. As the peril of overpopulation has become perceived and absorbed by the public and by the lawmakers, we have witnessed the total legalization of abortion. We have witnessed a historic change in the popular conception of a human fetus; it is no longer a "life," but rather, the mere possibility of one. Although religious institutions have been the slowest to react, we are also seeing changes in their doctrine. The very definition of "life" for the purpose of our laws against murder thus reflects a differential societal perception of the danger to human survival.

What of the more typical case of "murder"? Why does our statute provide that a human being who kills another shall forfeit his own life? If capital punishment is appropriate in our modern age of an overpopulated world, how could it ever have been appropriate in conditions of perceived underpopulation? Capital punishment was conceived for the purpose of deterrence. Even in an underpopulated society, the best way to ensure the minimum number of intentional killings is to threaten the killer with the loss of his own life. Unfortunately, in those few cases where the threat fails, society must exact capital punishment *not* because it has "promised" to do so or because vengeance is necessary, but rather—and only—to ensure the threat's credibility to future potential murderers. We have historical examples where, despite the statute, the penalty is not exacted. In time of war, when there have been severe shortages of military personnel, a convicted murderer will not be executed but will be sent into the front lines. Society does not want to "waste" even convicted murderers when, by being sent to the front fighting lines, they will contribute to its survival.

The foregoing considerations serve to indicate the narrowness of my colleague Professor Wun's individualistic approach to the present case. He views the law of murder as analogous to the rules of a game. He is afraid that the game will be impaired if the game rule is not applied to the four men who killed Whetmore. But why does he not inquire into the purpose of this game? Why do we have a law against murder? What values are at stake? These are the questions that go totally ignored in the one-dimensional approach of my colleague.

Under the view that I have outlined, we should consider the five explorers trapped in the cave as a total society. We do not have to do this in the same somewhat artificial sense expressed by Judge Foster. Rather, we can consider as a fact that the group existence of the five men would be terminated entirely unless they undertook strong action.

To survive, they had to kill and eat one of their number. We might draw an analogy to an individual who has to amputate a diseased limb that would otherwise threaten to destroy his body. (Similarly, the "body politic" in the cave had to kill one of its members to preserve the corpus.) As important as a leg or arm is to an individual, he or she should not hesitate to amputate it if that is the only way to preserve the life of the body. And, I might add, it is not essential to my analogy that the arm or leg be diseased. If one's limb were hopelessly trapped beneath a railroad tressle, amputation to avoid being killed by an oncoming train would be gruesome, but entirely rational. No religious prohibition of self-mutilation could make any sense in such a case. But then how can Professor Wun think that what the explorers did was in any sense immoral?

To the contrary, the most immoral act that we can conceive would be to terminate the life of the group. Conversely, one of the highest acts of morality is to preserve the life of a group. The explorers trapped in the cave must have sensed the force of this moral imperative. Despite all their previous training and all their previous social experiences and learned taboos, they had to reach the decision to engage in cannibalism in order to survive.

I could end my argument at this point, but perhaps it might be helpful for avoiding misunderstanding to spell out the acceptable procedures for implementing this moral imperative. Had one of the explorers been the "leader" in the cave, I would see nothing wrong with that leader *selecting* the victim whose flesh would provide the life-saving nutriment to the others. I would not second-guess the selection. Fairness in selection is as unimportant when the life of the group is at stake as it would be absurd, in my self-mutilation hypothetical, to have to be "fair" to all one's fingers if one of them has to be sacrificed. Thus the leader in the cave might base his selection of a victim on a ground as arbitrary as that suggested by Judge Tatting: Kill the one person who believes in afterlife, since the harm to him would be the least. Or it might be to kill the oldest, or the poorest, or—I hesitate to say it—the fattest. Or—to take care of Professor Wun's position—the decision might be to kill any individual who did not want to participate in the plan for group survival. Indeed, it would make no difference to me if the leader were to "reward" the person who *first proposed* the idea of cannibalism as a means of saving four out of five lives by selecting him as the victim.

Now, in fact, there was a "leadership" principle working in the cave, manifesting itself in the form of a democracy rather than an autocracy. The leadership was that of the group; its will became the ruling principle. It decided, in its wisdom, to give Roger Whetmore an even chance with the others in the throw of the dice. I do not consider that to have been a necessary part of the selection procedure, but the democratic nature of the proceedings in the cave certainly does not hurt my overall argument. Perhaps the "leadership" that emerged in the cave could only have emerged if it were grounded, as it was, upon conditions of fairness and equality. No matter. The fact is that four men survived. Had the leadership principle not emerged, the rescue party would have found in the cave five dead speluncean explorers. Would such a scene have been fair repayment for the tremendous efforts of the rescue party? Yet those who now want to execute the group of the crime of self-preservation would essentially recreate such a scene.

There has been no violation of N.C.S.A. (N.S.) § 12-A stating that "[w]hoever shall willfully take the life of another shall be punished by death," since we must construe "life" as the life of the group in the cave, as we would in a situation where the entire society's future existence is imperiled. It is with the greatest irony, then, that we must conclude that the only person in this case who could violate the statute would be the public executioner, if he is allowed to proceed to execute the four defendants. He *would* be "willfully taking the life of another." As Chief Executive, you need not be an instrumentality in the derivation of an immoral conclusion from absurd premises. I urge you to pardon the defendants.

Opinion of Professor Thri

I recommend that you commute the sentence of the four defendants to several years' compulsory service in a hospital or similar place where they can help save the lives of others, for I believe that the defendants are neither guilty nor innocent of the crime of murder. Lest my position appear to compromise between those of my colleagues, I hasten to point out at the outset that no true compromise between their extreme positions appears possible. They present a thesis and an antithesis on what constitutes "life." Even so, I want to draw upon aspects of each of their separate opinions in constructing my own synthesis.

Let me start with Professor Tieu's argument that the relevant unit in this case is the group and not the individual. As she well knows from our many discussions, I reject the metaphysics upon which she leans in fashioning a larger-than-life portrait of the group or the state. But metaphysics aside, I find her present argument nothing other than the old, and I should have thought discredited, philosophy of utilitarianism.

A classic objection to this form of utilitarianism is that in practice it becomes the tyranny of the majority. A society may, for example, enslave members of a different race, and then justify the continued system of slavery on the ground that the harm to a minority (the enslaved) is outweighed by the happiness and luxury afforded to the majority (the citizenry). There is a similar danger in Professor Tieu's espousal of the arbitrary grounds for selecting the explorers' victim. If Whetmore were selected arbitrarily, the procedure would be as morally unjustifiable as the perversion of utilitarianism that justifies slavery. I think Professor Tieu's argument would be improved if she required that each person in the cave be subjected to an equal chance of being killed. In that permutation we might see utilitarianism in its pure form.

But even with the proviso of fairness in the selection of the victim, her argument would still be vulnerable. Suppose a crime is committed which causes great public outrage, and many lives will be lost in riots if the killer is not apprehended and brought to justice quickly. If the police cannot find the killer, utilitarianism requires that the authorities select an innocent person as a scapegoat, manufacture evidence, and convict him. Many lives would be saved at the expense of one, although the law is perverted. Similarly, utilitarianism would condone Professor Wun's organ-transplant hypotheticals, which save several lives at the expense of one. Since all these examples are logically required by utilitarianism, we can only conclude that the philosophy does not express a moral system.

But despite my criticisms of Professor Tieu's philosophical premises, I want now to derive an important argument from her insistence upon the group as the relevant unit. Her simplistic vision of the "group" usefully summarizes a complex set of mutual reliances. The explorers were in fact engaged in a cooperative enterprise. In general, when a person decides to join a society to go spelunking in the company of its members he knows by the very nature of its being a joint expedition that the others will support him if a common danger or emergency arises. Indeed, this is why explorers tend to work in groups. A solitary explorer would be taking enormous risks of being disabled and being unable to summon help. Even in a two-person exploring team, if one is hurt and needs continuous attention, there would be no third person to summon assistance. We can readily see that important safety increments may be added as each marginal person joins the group. We might well infer that in the absence of any other evidence, Whetmore's decision to go exploring with the others may have been critical in their decision to go exploring at all. They may have decided that safety considerations required five; and, impliedly, all five would have to undertake to pitch in to ensure group safety. In short, Professor Tieu is right in her criticism of Professor Wun's "zero-sum game" approach. Clearly the explorers were not engaged in a mutually antagonistic or competitive enterprise going into the cave or even when the landslide sealed off the passage.

It is this sense that a coherent meaning can be given to the charge by the four defendants that Whetmore was guilty of a "breach of faith" when he withdrew from the lottery. Professor Wun assumes the charge was based solely upon Whetmore's withdrawing from the lottery after having suggested it was the right thing to do. But a more reasonable explanation of their charge is that Whetmore had no right not to contribute to the solution of the emergency that threatened all of them, just as he would have had no right to refuse to take his turn at chopping through the wall of the cave if that had been a feasible means of escape. When he joined the group, Whetmore knew that he was committing himself to *full participation* in the event of emergency. If Whetmore at the outset of the exploration had declared that if he was not in the mood when an emergency arose he would feel no obligation to do his share in helping to meet it, we can be quite certain that the others would not have accepted him as part of their group.

If Whetmore had no right to withdraw from the group's attempt to meet the emergency, does it follow that the defendants had a right to include him in their lottery and to kill him when he emerged the loser? If I could answer this question affirmatively, I would reach the same result as Professor Tieu and conclude that the defendants are innocent of any crime. However, the argument stops short of fully convincing me because of the following objection.

In joining the group Whetmore implicitly agreed to do his share of the work and to participate in the handling of emergency situations. Thus if the combined effort of five men could have moved the boulders that sealed the cave, he would have had no right to refuse to participate. But there are two limits, each decisive, to the inferred agreement to participate in an emergency. First, joint exploration does not require that any person be required to risk his *life* to save the others. Such an act of moral altruism is rare in any circumstance and certainly has never been a part of normal expected behavior. A mountain climber, for example, might slip and be placed in mortal danger; the others in the group must do everything to help her save herself, but they are not expected to risk their lives to save hers. (Of course, I am talking of a meaningful risk of life, and not a negligible one which might indeed be present in any exploring venture; in fact, I am talking about a 20% risk of life, which was the chance in the lottery in the present case.) Second, even if we concede that the explorers agreed to risk their lives to save another in an emergency, the situation in the cave was entirely beyond their agreement. In the normal case a risk is undertaken in which all might be saved. Rescuer and rescued combine to overcome a situation so that both will survive. But in the cave the explorers had passed that point. The boulders were unmovable. Nature had already won. Indeed, the exploring enterprise was over, for no amount of effort, no degree of risk against nature could make any difference. It was inconsistent with the idea of a lottery that everyone could survive. Therefore such a situation was not at all contemplated in the agreement to go exploring. Whetmore had not lost the right to choose not to be a part of a pact that would result in certain death "by inference" when he originally agreed to go exploring. It is clear that unless another argument is made on behalf of the defendants, the "group" argument is insufficient to exonerate them.

But such an argument can be made, I believe, if we examine closely the reasoning relating to the defense of "necessity" in Professor Wun's opinion. Professor Wun disclaims total opposition to the "necessity" argument. Clearly his own hypothetical example of Whetmore finding food pills in the pickaxe handle is a compelling case for allowing such a defense. This Commonwealth certainly recognizes that each human being has a privilege, if survival is at stake, to appropriate the property of another. It is a property-for-life case, and the defendants in the pickaxe hypothetical would have a legal right to take the pills by force, so long as they left Whetmore enough pills so that he could survive.

The problem that I have with my colleague's reasoning is his easy assumption that the speluncean explorers is a life-for-life case. My colleague argues that when Whetmore told the others that he had withdrawn from the scheme, they could have excluded Whetmore and proceeded to work out a suicide pact among themselves. Accordingly, one of the four would lose and would have killed himself. The three would be entitled to eat his dead flesh, and Whetmore, having excluded himself from the total arrangement, would not be so entitled. But here is the flaw in my colleague's reasoning. At that point Whetmore *would* be entitled to eat the nutriment, since it is no longer a "life" but is merely the "property" of the other three explorers. The fact that his withdrawal from the lottery was conditioned upon his subsequent disentitlement to partake of the nutriment is nothing other than a statement that the other three explorers have a property interest in the dead body. Yet this interest can legally be overcome when a life (Whetmore's) is at stake, just as in the pickaxe example a property interest in the pills can be overcome when survival is at stake.

We can well imagine what would happen a day or two after one of the four explorers died and the others are surviving on his dead flesh. Whetmore might beg for food, he might repent his "ill-advised" decision not to participate in the lottery, and he would surely point out that there is ample food for all to survive for ten more days, and that their insistence upon excluding him now would mean that he would die when he could otherwise survive at no cost to them. An argument exists for Whetmore to the effect that the others will be guilty of murder if they deprive him of the nutriment. For if he has a legal right to the nutriment—a right based upon the property-for-life argument from "necessity"—then they have no right to deprive him of it. Such a deprivation would in fact amount to murder.

Thus we arrive at the conclusion that there was no way legally for the others to exclude Whetmore from surviving on the dead flesh of one of their number. Or to put it differently, at the moment Whetmore withdrew from the lottery, he was in effect, if not consciously, trying to ensure his own survival at no risk to himself. Clearly the law cannot single out one person for special treatment, requiring the others to risk their own lives to save Whetmore. Conversely, the others were legally justified in forcibly including him in their lottery.

We now have the argument in behalf of the defendants. First, the "group" argument operates to show that they had a right *to some extent* to rely upon Whetmore's participation. Second, the "necessity" argument indicates that there was no reasonable nor fair alternative to their forcibly including Whetmore in the lottery. But while these two arguments distinguish the present case from Professor Wun's organ-transplant hypotheticals, the defendants are not completely innocent. They took a life, and they profited from it; technically, they violated the statute. Yet if it ever made sense to have a pardoning power, it makes sense to have it in a case of technical violation of statute where a substantial justification can be advanced for the violation. And the pardoning power is not an all-or-nothing tool. The defendants' sentences can be commuted to *lesser* penalties. I would urge that the defendants be sentenced to three or four years' compulsory service in a hospital or similar institution where they may be in a position to save the lives of people who need help. In that fashion, I believe, exact justice will have been achieved.

CHAPTER SEVEN. JUSTICE

The previous two chapters contained an account of the mythical, fascinating Case of the Speluncean Explorers. As we look back at that case, we see that the law itself set up a dilemma for the judges. The law gave the judges an all-or-nothing choice with nothing in between. The law said to the judges, "you can either free these defendants, or send them to be executed, but nothing in between." The law knew no alternative between innocent and guilty.

This sharp dichotomy, this discontinuity between innocent and guilty, is what generated the philosophical outpourings of the judges. They were faced with a Hobson's choice—either alternative is bad. And so they turned to jurisprudential rationalizations.

The last decision-maker, Professor Thri, refused to accept the dichotomy that the law thrust upon him. Instead, he recommended a sentence that would neither free the defendants nor execute them. If this course of action strikes you as the most just, then you can see the tension between the law and justice.

But that tension is most often a figment of the imagination. "Law" is not necessarily opposed to justice. "Law" may instead be thought of as the resolution of conflict situations according to justice. The situations themselves may have "law" in them, but the resolution of the situations can accord with justice as opposed to the purely verbal elements we call "law."

This concept is not easy to explicate in the abstract. Let us consider an extended, but simple, example.

Suppose your friend is driving someone to the hospital who has just had a heart attack or a stroke, and getting there in a hurry is a matter of life and death. She decides to drive through red lights on her way to the hospital. Later she tells you that on her way she was stopped by a police car for speeding, and although the police speedily took the heart-attack victim to the hospital, they gave her a speeding ticket anyway. Imagine that you are a lawyer and have to represent your friend in traffic court.

Perhaps the argument that you should NOT make to the court is the following: "Your honor, it is only fair and just that my client be allowed to go through the red lights because of the emergency situation." True, it is an argument based on "justice," but it implicitly pits justice against the law! You're saying that justice represents the reason your client went through the red lights, but the law is the red light itself which commands vehicles to stop on the red signal. A positivist would say that law is one thing and justice another, but that is not a good reason for you to make such an argument in court when you're trying to win a case based on justice. You can well imagine the judge saying, "Your client deliberately went through a red light. She may have had a good reason, but most people who go through a red light believe they had a good reason for doing so. My job is to dispense equal justice. It is only fair that I treat everyone the same. Everyone who goes through a red light is guilty in my courtroom."

The argument you would be better off making is one that demonstrates that the law itself contains justice. You should contend that the only way to interpret the law rationally is to make sure that the law brings out the justice that is inherent in it. The argument might proceed as follows:

"Your honor, traffic signals were set up by the legislature to impose reasonable and readily ascertainable standards for orderly traffic control in the normal case. The legislature knew that a red light is an imperfect instrument, not responsive to every situation but generally useful for most situations. Sometimes a red light can malfunction and get stuck; everyone knows that the cars don't have to remain stopped for several hours until someone repairs the red light. And everyone knows this because it has become obvious, at that point, that the red light has failed the very purpose for which it was set up, which is to effect a reasonable and orderly control of traffic.

"There are other situations to which even a perfectly functioning red light is not responsive. The red light is certainly not responsive to the situation where a police car has to go through the red light. Nor is it responsive to ambulances. My client in the present case fits into this category of exceptional situations. The legislature could not have intended that a passenger die in a car of a heart attack because the driver had to stop at red lights on the way to the hospital. We know that the legislature could not have intended this, because their very purpose in setting up the red lights in the first place was to minimize the loss of life or the danger to life that is an ever-present danger in this age of motorized vehicles. The legislature wanted to minimize the loss of life, not increase it. Clearly the legislators of this state would not have intended that a red light be responsible for the death of a heart-attack victim being driven to a hospital. Yet science has not yet made it possible for the legislature to work out a system whereby the red light itself could sense when a vehicle was on the way to the hospital. The red light cannot know when a vehicle is an ambulance or a fire engine or a police car. The red light cannot know when someone in a private automobile is being rushed to the hospital in a life-threatening situation. And so the legislature relied instead upon the good sense and judgment of the courts of law. They knew that judges would understand these exceptional cases. They knew that judges would not close their eyes to the exceptional cases and simply rule against every driver without exception who went through a red light, because if judges did that, your honor, judges would be no different and no better than red lights. Courts would blink on and off mechanically the way red lights do, instead of correcting the artificial imperatives of the traffic lights.

"What I am contending, your honor, is that the legislature counted on the presence of a humane and rational court system when it enacted its traffic-control regulations. It was able to demarcate clear lines because it knew that courts would supply the necessary flexibility. It was able to rule that cars must stay in their proper lanes and not cross the double white line in the middle of the road because the legislature knew that in emergencies—for instance, if a child runs out into the street—a driver who avoided hitting the child by crossing the double white line would not then be arrested for violating a traffic command. Or if he were arrested, the court would not find him guilty of a traffic violation, but rather the court would instruct the arresting officer that lives are more important than white lines.

"The legislature, then, did not enact its statutes in a vacuum. Rather, the legislature knew that there was a court system out there, a system which would look at the purposes for which the statutes were enacted and then interpret the statutes in light of those purposes. The purpose of traffic regulations is to save lives and minimize accidents. When that purpose conflicts with a particular traffic regulation—such as the double white line and the darting child, or the red light and the person being rushed to the hospital—then the courts step in to ensure that the purpose is fulfilled. If the literal meaning of the statute conflicts with the purpose in a given case, such as an emergency case, then so much the worse for the literal meaning. The legislature did not intend to enact literal meanings; rather, the legislature intended to use statutes to fulfill its legislative purposes.

"Statutes are no good without courts. Statutes and courts work together to effectuate the legislative purpose. And this is exactly what the legislature intended when it enacted the statutes. My client instinctively knew this by deciding to save the life of the passenger even at the risk of being arrested for a minor infraction of the law. What I am now arguing is that the police officer should not have arrested my client, that what my client did is clearly not an infraction of the law, and that this case should not have come to this busy court in the first place. But now that it is before you, I am arguing that you take this opportunity to inform the public, and the arresting officer, that the law is not a blind mechanism. The public should be informed that, in dire emergencies, reasonable exceptions to traffic control laws will be allowed by courts of law. Of course, the emergency has to be real, as it is in this case; and this court will always exist to make sure that the emergency in fact was a genuine one. All I am asking this court to do is to apply the traffic-control statute in exactly the way the legislature intended it to be applied, no more no less, that is, by supplying the vision that the red light itself could not have—the knowledge that this driver was complying with the real purpose of the traffic-control laws in acting reasonably to save the life of a fellow human being."

That was a long-winded argument, a bit pompous for such an insignificant case, but I spelled it out to indicate how the normative force of justice considerations can be utilized in an argument based not directly upon justice but upon existential statutory materials. The argument is an attempt to show that the law itself exists not to rule us literally but rather to effectuate justice. Justice in the traffic-control context is equivalent to saving lives and avoiding accidents.

I do not claim that the foregoing argument is a winner in any traffic court. I'm not saying that if you repeat it some day when you're trying to get out of a ticket that it will work for you. But I am suggesting, out of my own litigating experience and my study of the law, that it is the kind of argument that utilizes the normative dimension of law in a way that a judge can accept.

A. POSITIVISM AND THE SEPARATION THESIS

The positivists, as we have seen in previous chapters, are uncomfortable with the idea that law contains justice. They argue instead that law is one thing and justice something different. Of course, they quickly add, justice considerations often act as an influence upon the law. But they emphatically deny that there is any intrinsic relation between law and justice.

The most central tenet of positivism, in my view, is the claim that law and justice are separate from each other. I call this the "Separation Thesis." I want to explain what it is and then try to refute it.

Positivists don't often call attention to what I have labelled the "Separation Thesis." But the thesis arises in protean disguises throughout law and litigation. Part of a lawyer's task is to recognize the separation thesis when it is implicitly asserted in a legal argument or debate. Often a tip-off comes from the use of the common word "irrelevant." When an attorney attempts to point to a consideration that the court ought to take into account, opposing counsel might object on the ground that such a consideration is "irrelevant." Many times when this objection arises, what is really happening is an assertion of the Separation Thesis.

The word "irrelevant" is, after all, just a claim that some facts and some arguments should be heard by the court and others should not be heard. But often the arguments that are shunned by the term "irrelevant" are precisely those that point up the injustice of the other side's position. "Irrelevant" is often nothing more than a restatement of the Separation Thesis.

How did the Separation Thesis get started? Positivists contend that law is a fact, and as such, it cannot be the same thing as a normative value. They say that any law can be criticized according to the critic's own values—for example, any person can say that a given law is unjust. But it is still the law, whether just or unjust.

Thus, positivists claim that only confusion results if we try to intermingle law and values.

At the center of positivism are two basic propositions: (1) a fact cannot logically give rise to a value consideration such as justice, and (2) law is a fact. Because positivism accepts both of these basic propositions, it concludes that law does not necessarily include justice—that justice does not necessarily inform the law. This conclusion is another way of stating the Separation Thesis.

Let us begin by a critical examination of basic proposition (1), the logical argument that a fact cannot give rise to a value. We will use the logical term "entail" to mean "logically compel" or "give rise to." Consider the following logical argument (syllogism):

1. A fetus is a human life in being.
2. Abortion is an operation that kills a fetus.
3. Abortion is the killing of a human life.

Does the combination of sentences 1 and 2 entail sentence 3? Yes. Sentence 3, the conclusion, is therefore logically "valid." This does not mean that sentence 3 is true. The truth of sentence 3 depends on the truth of sentences 1 and 2. If either 1 or 2 were false, 3 would then be false, even though 3 is logically entailed by 1 and 2. You can see this by the following syllogism:

1A. A fetus is not a human life in being.
2. Abortion is an operation that kills a fetus.
3A. Abortion is not the killing of a human life.

This syllogism is also valid. Sentences 1A and 2 entail conclusion 3A.

In proper debate, however, one can often discern propositions of the following form:

1B. A fetus is a human life in being.
3B. Abortion is an operation that kills a fetus.
4B. One ought not to commit nor allow an abortion.

But it is clear that the "ought" in sentence 4B is not entailed by sentences 1B and 3B. As the philosopher David Hume demonstrated, factual premises cannot entail a moral conclusion. We need another sentence to make the syllogism valid:

> 2B. One ought not to take a human life.

You might say that sentence 2B is implied in sentence 1B. In other words, you might argue that if we conclude that a fetus is a human life in being, we are impliedly asserting sentence 2B. Yet many of the misunderstandings in popular debate may be traced to the assumption that certain premises are implied. It is always best to state one's premises clearly so that we might see exactly whether the stated form is what is implied or meant. Thus, sentence 2B cannot always be true. Human lives are taken in war; human lives are taken when capital punishment is imposed; and sometimes human lives are taken in order to save other human lives. Suppose we revised sentence 2B into the following sentence 2C:

> 2C. One ought not to take a human life except when absolutely necessary.

If we did, then conclusion 4C would follow:

> 4C. One ought not to commit nor allow an abortion except when absolutely necessary.

This, of course, is quite a different conclusion from 4B.

We live in a universe of fact. Nature proceeds in its course "red in tooth and claw." Animals kill and eat other animals for food. Volcanoes erupt and wipe out populations; towns can be destroyed by floods; a succession of dry seasons can bring famines that can destroy civilizations. Primitive people used to look at these violent manifestations of nature and interpret them as punishments inflicted by angry gods for evildoing in their own villages. But our own perspective on these events is simply that we live on a fragile green planet in a minor solar system in one of billions of galaxies. Storms and floods occurred throughout the history of earth, long before there were people. The evolution of life up to the era of the dinosaurs seemed to end, long before there were humans, in the strongest form of life, yet sixty million years ago all the dinosaurs perished, perhaps as the result of the impact of a huge meteor that collided with the earth causing debris that darkened the skies for years, creating super-cold conditions that wiped out the dinosaurs.

Nearly everyone agrees with Hume that a mere fact of nature cannot itself entail a value. Just because something exists is no reason why it ought to exist. The AIDS virus exists, but that fact cannot stand as a reason why we should not try to eradicate it. In short, we cannot construct a system of morality simply by looking at the facts in the universe. In order to get to a moral conclusion, we have to interpret those facts morally. Of course, once we do so, we are putting morality in our premises; then moral conclusions will be entailed. When we added sentences 2C and 2D above, we were putting moral interpretations into the premises of our syllogisms. Only by doing so could we derive moral conclusions.

Therefore, we have accepted basic proposition (1) of positivism; that a fact or facts cannot logically entail moral values such as justice. But we now have to face basic proposition (2) of the positivists, that law is a value-free fact. If law is a fact, then justice cannot necessarily be part of the law. For justice is a moral value, and moral values, as we have seen, cannot logically be entailed by mere statements of fact. Thus, if we are to refute positivism, we must attack their basic proposition (2).

Putting law aside for the moment, can we think of any factual statement that embodies a value? Professor Hilary Putnam says that the following two are examples of millions of possible statements of that sort:

1) Yeats was a great poet.
2) The Nazis were evil.[1]

Of course, one might *dispute* that Yeats was a great poet, but that does not mean that the statement is not factual.[2]

Is law a fact? Certainly in the following trivial example it is: We might say that a particular statute was passed on January 10, 1937, by majority vote in both houses of Congress, and enacted on January 15 when President Roosevelt signed it. That much is a fact. Or we might

[1] H. Putnam, *The Many Faces of Realism* 63 (1987).

[2] One can dispute the statement "At the present moment, there are exactly 13,783,982 red-headed persons living in the United States," but it is nevertheless a factual statement.

say that *Smith v. Jones* is a decided case because it appears on page 239 of volume 87 of the Illinois Reports. But aren't these only records of law, or evidences of law? Isn't the law itself a set of immaterial standards, intangible norms, and learned processes of reaching decisions in respect of factual situations? Isn't law a product of the human mind rather than something that exists in the state of nature?

More than that, isn't law addressed to the shaping and controlling of human behavior? Doesn't it exist only because of its efficacy in making an impact upon the decisions that we choose in everyday life? We saw in Chapter One that law would make no sense if it did not channel human behavior in socially desirable directions. Law exerts an immaterial, but nevertheless potent, impact upon our decisional processes. True, law does not control our decisions; sometimes people simply disobey the law. But there would be no point in studying law if it did not have an influence upon human behavior.

Influences upon our behavior may nevertheless be morally neutral. The weather influences our behavior, yet it is a morally neutral phenomenon (except, perhaps, in the minds of primitive societies). Law, simply considered as an influence upon our behavior, may be justice-neutral.

But justice and morality come into the picture because law is enforced by human beings. If Mr. Jones disobeys the law, the police may step in and arrest Mr. Jones. Or Mr. Smith may sue Mr. Jones. As a result of the arrest or lawsuit, Mr. Jones may be forced to pay a penalty. This penalty may be forcibly extracted from Mr. Jones by the sheriff. And behind the sheriff stands the armed might of the state. Hence, in the enforcement of law, some human beings (judges, sheriffs, the army) may forcibly interfere in the lives of other human beings (those who violate the law).

Now we have more than an abstract "influence" upon behavior. We have actual, or potential, physical interference by some human beings in the lives of other human beings. When some human beings thus purport to interfere in the freedom of other human beings, they typically demand justificatory arguments in support of that interference.

In the case we considered where the driver went through red lights in order to speed a person to the hospital, we saw that judges will tend to respond to justificatory arguments. But consider the police officer who arrested the driver. He might explain, "I'm giving you a traffic ticket for a good reason. The reason is that you went through the red light." A positivist might applaud. For positivists believe that the "reason" officials enforce the law is the content of the law that they enforce.

These positivist "reasons" appear to be restatements of the positivist assumption that law is a fact. If one asks why the law is as it is, the positivists reply with another fact—that the law was duly enacted by the legislature.

But an entirely different result emerges if we challenge the assumption that the rule cited by the policeman is a mere fact. The argument I suggested to the traffic-court judge merges law and justice. The law embodies justice; justice thus gives shape to our interpretation of the law.

Is there any way that the positivist might respond to the previous argument? By rigidly invoking the separation thesis, a positivist might argue to the judge: "Your honor, this driver undoubtedly did the right thing in speeding to the hospital. I'm the first person to say that all of us should act at all times in accordance with our own sense of justice and morality. But the traffic regulation that applied to this case makes no exceptions for going through the red light. This court should apply the law as it is written and not as it might want the law to be written. As it is written, drivers of private automobiles must stop at the red light. The penalty for disobedience is a fine of $50. This court has no discretion in the matter; it must apply the law that the legislature has enacted. Clearly this driver did not obey the law. Of course, this driver disobeyed the law for a good reason. The reason is worth more than the $50 fine. And so, your honor, you should find this driver guilty of shooting the red lights, and impose a penalty of $50. That is a small price for the driver to pay for the satisfaction of saving the life of a passenger."

What rejoinder can we make to the positivist's argument. Consider the following: "Your honor, my client can afford to pay the $50, but as a matter of principle my client should not be convicted of a misdemeanor, even a very small one such as this. My client is a law-abiding person. The traffic regulations as a whole are designed to avoid accidents, and what my client did was to help save a life and avoid the accidental death that might come to the passenger by not speeding him to the hospital."

Now our positivist replies: "If the legislature wanted to pass a statute that simply said, 'drive in such a way as to avoid accidents,' the legislature would have done so. Instead, the legislature decided to make specific traffic regulations. The court's job is to apply these specific regulations."

Now how would you reply? Consider this: "Your honor, if you impose fines on all drivers who go through red lights in order to rush a heart-attack victim to the hospital, you will eventually teach the public to stop at red lights no matter what the cost, because the public as a whole wants to obey the law. And the result of training drivers never to shoot the lights will some day result in more losses of life than to be flexible about the matter."

The positivist judge cannot dispute this argument, because he knows that law does have an impact upon behavior—an impact that in some cases overrides a person's moral impulses. Not everyone will disobey the law in order to vindicate a moral principle; many people if faced with such a dilemma will comply with the law. So the judge is forced to answer as follows: "If what you say does occur, the legislature will hear about it, and will be forced, under public pressure, to amend the traffic regulations so as to provide an exception to the red signal rule. When they enact an exception that allows drivers to shoot the lights for emergency reasons, then I will faithfully apply that exception in cases such as yours. But until then, you have violated the law."

The judge, in short, is willing to risk foreseeable accidents in order to bring pressure on the legislature to modify their rule. This was Judge Keen's approach to the necessity defense in the Speluncean Explorers' Case: changes in the law are matters for the legislature, not the courts. But why should the judge have such a narrow conception of his own duty in the matter? Why should the judge feel duty-bound to apply a law which, under his own theory, is simply a value-free fact? What conception does he have of the office of judge that would lead him to accept the death of a person who needs hospital care as a price for getting the law changed? What moral force exists in a value-free law that would override the judge's moral responsibility to unnamed heart-attack victims? Would the legislature itself want judges to apply rules so rigidly? Would the legislature be happy reading about a driver who dutifully stopped at a red light while his passenger's heart stopped beating? Wouldn't the legislature criticize the judge for teaching the community such a mechanical interpretation of the law?

There is no adequate reason why the judge should feel an obligation to apply a value-free rule when its application can result in the potential death of an innocent person. And that is why most judges, in practice, would not convict the driver. Indeed, it is why most policemen would not give the driver a ticket in the first place.

Our example has been a peculiar one, designed to test the underpinnings of positivist theory. While it brings out the need for enforcers of the law to have justificatory arguments, the example fortunately is not representative of real-world situations of judicial behavior.

We see in this example that positivism itself is a self-actualizing theory. If a judge starts with the premise that laws are morally neutral, he may consistently arrive at a result such as finding the driver guilty even while praising the driver's moral courage in violating the law. But such a premise also requires the judge to attempt to shift the responsibility for tragic applications of the law to the legislature. Such a shifting of responsibility comes at the cost of encouraging—by the rigid application of rules—a number of unavoided tragic deaths. Is there any good reason for a judge to constrict himself so much, to wear moral blinders, just to enforce a law which the judge claims is value-free? If there is no good reason for a judge to do that, then can there be any good reason to adopt the Separation Thesis in the first place? The Separation Thesis is not a description of law; rather, it is simply a first premise, a postulate. May we not reject the Separation Thesis if, for us, it fails to explain judicial behavior?

Law regulates human conduct and serves to justify the imposition of penalties upon people for behavior contrary to law. Since law has this overwhelming, comprehensive purpose, and since a justificatory reason always seems to be necessary to account for why judges and sheriffs apply and enforce the law, may we not conclude that arguments of justice are intrinsic to the law? In other words, may we not conclude that the Separation Thesis is invalid?

B. JUSTICE AND LEGISLATION

When we look at all the rules in a society, we can come across particular rules that seem to be unjust. In what sense then can we argue that those particular rules contain justice or are inherently connected to justice?

One distinction we should make is between macro-justice and micro-justice. Micro-justice means that every single rule is just. This is an impossible ideal; no society will consist solely of perfectly just rules. The concept of macro-justice, on the other hand, recognizes that some rules and regulations will be unjust to some groups, and others will be unjust to other groups. The system is in a state of macro-justice if all these injustices more or less cancel each other out. For instance, a progressive income tax may appear to be unjust to high-income taxpayers. But the system may also have a sales tax, which is for the most part regressive and hence favors those high-income taxpayers. The combination of the two taxes, each unfair but to a different group, might have a cancelling-out effect when considered from a macro-justice perspective.

Another possibility is that some laws will be unjust without destroying the over-all contention that justice is at the basis of legislation in general. Suppose Oregon passes a vehicle safety act that specifically exempts lumber-carrying trucks. These trucks, which sometimes are the equivalent length of three buses, carry enormous logs from lumber camps to processing mills. An accident victim of a lumber truck that was unable to stop in the normal time that other vehicles could stop would probably say that it was unjust to exempt these trucks from the safety regulations. The victim might also be able to point to special-interest lobbying that led to the exemption passed by the state legislature for the lumber industry. Would that mean that the exemption was unjust? Not necessarily. The public might be sufficiently dependent economically on the lumber industry to make it fair for the public to decide to absorb some vehicular accidents rather than to pass legislation that might make it competitively impossible for the lumber industry in Oregon to stay in business.

Whether we are considering legislation or judicial precedents, "justice" seems to have formed a part of their creation and hence "justice" seems relevant in interpreting their applicability to the issue at hand. The Separation Thesis, after all, is not itself a Law embodied in our Constitution. Rather, it is simply a theory of law. It has a certain immediate appeal—because it is easier for people to think of the world of facts and the world of values as two different worlds, than to engage in the intellectually more difficult task of understanding that they are simply two perspectives on one world—the world we actually have. When we look at the legal world, we see that laws are *incomplete* if we interpret them solely as facts, and equally *incomplete* if we interpret them solely as values. The Separation Thesis requires us to distinguish between two things that are aspects of the same phenomenon—something akin to distinguishing between procedure and substance in the law when we know that procedure and substance are constantly and inevitably interacting with each other all the time.

Since many people—especially judges—subconsciously accept some degree of separation between law and justice, lawyers should make a special effort to recognize the Separation Thesis when it is being played like background music, and to argue effectively for a change of tune. For the general reader, perhaps the hardest task is to rethink the relation between law and justice and not to assume that because they are two separate *words* they must be two separate concepts.

C. JUSTICE AND RHETORIC

Because positivism is such a pervasive philosophy in all of today's law in the United States and in English-speaking countries generally, it's natural to expect that judges have become imbued with positivist philosophy. Judges will tend to articulate the false dichotomy between law and justice that positivists want them to practice. For example, the plaintiff's attorney tries to argue in court, "your honor, my client deserves to win because justice is on her side." And the judge sarcastically responds, "and tell me what's on the defendant's side—the law?" If the judge says that, the plaintiff is doomed. The judge will invariably decide according to the law. The judge, having drawn a distinction between law and justice, will decide according to the law and leave the "justice" considerations to religion and social metaphysics.

Does the judge's response vindicate positivism after all? Should we conclude that, if law is a prediction of what courts will decide, and if judges are going to respond in that fashion, then maybe law and justice are distinct concepts? No, the problem began when the plaintiff's attorney argued that justice is on the plaintiff's side. Do you see why? *Implicit* in the attorney's argument was the contention that the only way the plaintiff was going to win was for the judge to rule in the plaintiff's favor for reasons of justice *despite* what the law said. And that is invariably a losing rhetorical strategy.

Attorneys who know something about legal philosophy wouldn't make such a mistake. Rather, they will use the "justice" considerations on the plaintiff's side of the case to shape the structure of the legal arguments that they present for the plaintiff. In all cases, there is always a legal argument to be made on each side (even in the extreme case where the only legal argument seems to be the argument that the controlling legal precedent ought to be overruled!)[3] The good attorney uses "justice" considerations to shape the way the legal arguments are presented, to inform their content, and to bundle them in a persuasive package. If justice is really on the plaintiff's side in a particular case, the plaintiff's attorney ought to be able to argue powerfully that the law compels a decision in the plaintiff's favor.

I've never encountered a judge who had no interest in doing justice. Doing justice is a powerful motive for judges charged with the fair administration of the law. But justice should never be presented to the court as an alternative to the law. Justice should be *implicit* in the choice and presentation of the legal materials that are used in a case.

[3] But arguments in court always have to be made in good faith. See Rule 11, Federal Rules of Civil Procedure. Thus, if the only argument that an attorney can make is that a controlling precedent ought to be overruled, the court will consider that a frivolous argument and subject to Rule 11 sanctions unless the attorney can in good faith show as a matter of law (using the "justice" arguments to structure that legal argument) that the precedent should be overruled.

D. JUSTICE AND LEGAL REALISM

At the beginning of Chapter Four, I suggested the notion of law as a prediction of what courts will decide, and said that the prediction theory grows out of the school of jurisprudential thought known as "legal realism." Legal realism is largely a twentieth-century American phenomenon, although actually its roots can be found in nineteenth century German legal philosophy. Legal realists say that there is a wide range of factors, some conscious and some subconscious, that influence judges in their decisions. Some are biological: the fact that judges used to be only men obviously had a lot to do with decisions denying equal rights to women. Some factors are political: the fact that judges today have good salaries and are respected in their communities may mean that on the whole these judges may be biased against poor people, or immigrants, or nonconformists.[4] Some factors may be personal: the judge may be feeling ill on judgment day and may thus be unduly harsh on whatever litigant happens to be there. A few years ago there was a New Yorker cartoon of a judge talking to another judge as they walked down the marble steps in front of the courthouse. The caption read, "Some days when I'm feeling rotten I sentence all the defendants to ten years; and other days when I'm feeling good, I give them six months. It all averages out."

I think that legal realism is accurate as far as it goes. Undoubtedly there are many factors that influence judicial decisions. And if my definition of law has been persuasive to you—that law is a prediction of judicial decisions—then we have to take legal realism into account in making those predictions and therefore in constituting what we mean by law.

But we are left with the troubling notion that some factors that might go into a judicial decision should *not* really count with judges. We are unwilling to say that law is *anything* that judges want it to be. In Chapter Four, we excluded some of these factors by the device of defining law, from the judge's point of view, as a prediction of what an average judge would decide—that is, a judge devoid of the

[4] The branch of legal realism that is particularly fashionable today in law-school circles is called "critical legal studies." Its concern is primarily with the underlying, macroscopic, and often subconscious "political" factors that pervade all of law.

particular judge's personal idiosyncracies. This approach takes us part of the way, but we still want to have some constraint upon the judge.

Suppose that *all* the judges in a jurisdiction are biased in favor of men. Then, even under the definition of law that I gave in Chapter Four, a particular judge might take into account this pervasive bias in his decision in a given case. So we need some other reference point that is external to all the judges in a jurisdiction.

Legal realism is hard put to come up with such an external reference point, since legal realism at best is only descriptive of what judges do. We need a *normative* external reference point. Of course, at this point in the book, there is no secret about what I think that external reference point is. I claim that justice acts as an external constraint upon judicial decisions. And since that is my claim, I think that a full-bodied theory of legal realism must take justice into account as a component of predicting what judges do and hence as a component of law itself.

Many legal realists would agree with me in principle, but what tends to block them from accepting my particular thesis about justice is their feeling that justice is a subjective phenomenon. They cannot see how or why a subjective phenomenon can be studied, defined, or used as an external reference point.

On the contrary, I suggest that we all share in a society-wide and to some extent world-wide consensus about justice. My proof of this proposition takes us to the final level of argument in this book.

E. THE OBJECTIVITY OF JUSTICE

The first and most important point to make about justice is that it *cannot* be defined in words. As soon as one attempts a verbal description of the content of justice, the result can be challenged and overturned. If I were to say that justice consists of giving every person what he deserves, all we have done is to substitute the ambiguous word "deserves" for the word "justice" and we are no further along. If I were to say that justice means "treating like cases alike and different cases differently," I might be coming closer to the elusive concept of justice but I still would be in trouble defining when cases are "alike." If instead I were to say that justice consists in giving every person food, clothing, and shelter, we might agree that the principle is fine but dispute the question where the food, clothing, and shelter will come from. For instance, if every person in the world today were given food, clothing, and shelter, and the cost of making those provisions would be charged against all persons who had any money or assets beyond the minimal food clothing and shelter, then all persons in developed countries such as the United States would immediately lose all their assets and be reduced to the poverty level. For there are so many people in the world who lack the basic necessities of life, that giving them those necessities would mean bankrupting everyone else. Now, maybe all people who have any money or assets should "give everything to the poor," as the New Testament says, but the problem arises when the state attempts forcibly to take away those assets and give them to the poor. The economic problem at bottom, consists of the fact that once everyone is reduced to subsistence, no one will have the incentive to produce a surplus since that surplus will then be confiscated. And the justice problem consists of the injustice of forcibly taking away property from people who have earned it.

Philosophers through the centuries have attempted to "define" justice, but in my view no one has succeeded. Theories of justice are readily available in the library, but they do not solve particular cases.

I suggest that we have to get away from a word-bound notion of justice. We should clear our minds of definitions and words, and look instead at the mental processes we go through when we make a judgment that a certain decision is just or unjust.

Let us then consider how a sense of justice arises and develops in our life histories. From our early childhood through the rest of our lives we are bombarded by competitive situations that come to our attention either because we see them, hear about them, or read about them, that human beings resolve one way or another. I use the term "competitive situation" generically as including all instances where two or more people want the same thing, where there is a "limited pie," where somebody wants something that somebody else has but is unwilling to give up (and either acts forcibly or simply makes a claim), where anyone is dissatisfied with his "share" of anything, where two or more people have a dispute over who should be assigned something that a third party is dispensing, and similar situations. In short, I am talking about human conflict generally. We learn, starting from childhood, how people resolve these conflicts. We can tell from the expressions on faces, gestures, words of anger, and so forth, whether contesting parties are satisfied or dissatisfied with various outcomes and what others do about such satisfaction or dissatisfaction. When we hear stories—and in childhood we hear many stories, see many "morality" plays on television, hear many sermons, and are told many cautionary tales—the storyteller usually makes it quite clear what the "right" outcome is of the recounted conflict situation. The "happy ending" is part of how we learn about justice.[5]

What counts for us as "similarities" are precisely those features of the many stories we hear that, for us, recur in other stories having the same outcomes. Our mental collection of remembered stories provides us, through the mental operation of similarity, with a sense of whether a decision in a new situation is fair or unfair.

The endless variety, the ceaseless bombardment of these stories and pictures and situations (many of which we find ourselves in), cannot be summarized in words. If anyone tried to summarize them, the summary would work, if at all, for the summarizer and not for anyone else. "Justice" is not definable; no amount of staring at it will tell you what it is. If two situations strike us as similar when we are going through the mental process of assessing them in accordance with our sense of justice, it is the similarity that may lead us to articulate a "rule" that links the two cases. My point is that the similarity comes first, not the rule. Thus the "rules"—the words, if you will—must be derivative and the similarities primitive.

Nor is justice static; if it were, then there might be an outside chance that a theorist might someday describe it. Instead, people evolve in their minds a continually refined sense of justice as they observe (read about, hear) more and more situations, notice the way these are resolved, and work out for themselves what the similarities are among these myriad situations that constitute a coherent sense of what the just outcomes are and should be. The culture as a whole does this, and hence there is a group evolution toward greater refinements in justice determinations.

[5] Recall that prior to the late 1950s Hollywood only released movies whose endings proved that crime did not pay.

My claim is that justice is real because it involves the way our minds work. If my claim is right, it follows that justice may constrain judicial decisions. If a judge wants to do justice to the parties in a case, then certain results, and not others, will be dictated by the application of remembered similarities to the case.

Such a far-reaching claim calls for empirical support. For in the absence of evidence that the mental processes labelled "justice" point in certain directions, one could concede the truth of everything I say but nevertheless introduce a fatal objection: the possibility that although each person "learns" about justice in the way I've described, each person might come out with a different, idiosyncratic answer. Unless there is a convergence of justice-answers across many observers, the entire mental process I've described may constrain one judge to decide one way but constrain a different judge to decide a different way. The end result would then be chaotic and not worth further pursuit.

I want to argue now that justice is objective. The empirical support for this proposition consists of an experiment that I want to do with you, the reader.

I ask you to consider the following situation: A mother of two children cuts the dessert cake; she hands a large piece to Steve and a small piece to Johnny. Is your sense of justice offended?

You will of course want to know what reason the mother offers for her decision. The sort of reason you are looking for is not a matter of words or rhetoric; for example, if the mother said that the transcendent nature of the universe as actualized by participants in the noosphere ordains giving Johnny the smaller piece, you would not be persuaded. But you can ask her to tell you the story of what facts and situations she had in mind when she made her decision. And you can compare these facts to all the similar situations you've encountered in your life and conclude whether the mother has violated your sense of justice. I claim that you will do these things even if you've never considered this particular problem before and even if you've never encountered stories of the kind that the mother tells.

Here are some of the mother's stories:

(a) "Stevie is handsomer."
(b) "Johnny looks exactly like a real nasty kid in the neighbor-

hood where I grew up."
(c) "Stevie cleaned his room but Johnny didn't."
(d) "The doctor put Johnny on a low sugar diet."
(e) "Because it's Tuesday."
(f) "Johnny hates cake."
(g) "They've got to learn that the world is a jungle."

When I tried these questions in my law-school course on Justice and the Legal System,[6] there was unanimity among the 44 students on every answer. They assigned the outcome "unjust" to reasons (a), (b), and (g). They awarded the outcome "just" to reasons (d) and (f). And as to (c) and (e), the class felt that the answer depended upon further information that was not given. There was no dissent when some students suggested the additional information that was needed and how it would change the result. Thus, as to (c), if Johnny truthfully says "yes, but I cleaned out the garage, which is what my mother asked me to do," then the initial impression of "just" as an answer to that story would change to "unjust." Or, as to (e), Tuesday appears to be a wholly arbitrary reason not to give Johnny an equal slice of cake, but if the mother's practice is to alternate larger shares every evening—that is, if Johnny got the larger slice on Monday and will again get it on Wednesday—then what first appeared to be an unjust" decision turns out to be "just."[7]

If you seriously dispute any of the preceding assignments of outcome, then my entire demonstration may fail as to you. I have considerable confidence that this will not happen. My confidence would be diminished if you came from a very different culture than

[6] "An experimental course that I am working out with Professor Arthur Jacobson of Cardozo Law School.

[7] This same mental experiment indicates the futility of trying to capture justice in theoretical terms. For simply noticing the mother giving the smaller piece of cake to Johnny does not allow us to imagine a complete set of all the factors that could go into the mother's decision to give him the smaller slice. The list of 7 reasons can obviously be expanded indefinitely, with infinite variations. No theory can be constructed that would generate or reflect all those variations. No theory can tell us finally what factors should be "relevant" to the mother's decision.

If it is impossible to construct a complete definition or a complete theory of justice that would specify how factors should be evaluated in order to do justice in dividing a cake for two children, it is obviously impossible to specify the justice principles for a complex society of millions of people. No matter what principles one may imagine, they cannot point to the correct results in all the cases that may arise. Indeed, they cannot point to the correct result in any single case.

most of the readers who are likely to read this book, but even then I think that a certain basic sense of justice is quite pervasive through the world.

Not only do I have confidence that the reader will adjudicate the cake outcomes the same way my students did, but I have the even greater expectation that no matter how many new kinds of factors the reader or anyone else invents for the mother in the cake example, there will be a similar convergence among adjudicators. This is indeed a far-reaching claim, for I am suggesting that factors and situations presented as reasons for the hypothetical mother that neither you nor I have ever thought about, whose possibilities we have never conceived, will lead to similar judgments on our part when we adjudicate the fairness of the mother's decision to give Stevie a larger slice of cake.[8] Surely, then, I have not made a word-bounded claim. If I am right, then you and I have a sense of justice that we somehow mentally "apply" to these situations even though we cannot possibly specify in words the content of that sense of justice. We cannot specify it since by definition we have not yet conceived of all the variable factors that will be presented to us.

"Justice," then, can have a definite meaning for us even if we cannot say in words what that meaning is. Our minds simply have "learned" to recognize similarities among situations and stories so that we can assign "justice" outcomes with considerable confidence. Moreover, we seem to do so effortlessly. Recall how you reacted to the variations on the sliced-cake problem. Did you start with some "text" in your mind that defined "justice," and then derive verbal hypotheses against the facts and compare the facts to the words and reach an articulate conclusion? My guess, instead, is that you simply "thought about" the problem by mentally conjuring up situational variations that you remember from your own experience and stories you've heard, and proceeded to visualize whether the outcomes were "fair" according to your way of thinking. Your mind compared

[8] I am not claiming that there cannot be close cases. Suppose the mother's reason is that "Johnny hasn't behaved as well as Stevie today," many observers looking at the actual facts of the matter might disagree with the mother. But I do make the claim that when the cases are "close," observers will agree that the cases are "close"! In close cases one observer might disagree with another as to the outcome, but both will recognize the plausibility of disagreement.

the similarities in the sliced-cake instances to other situations you've encountered in your life (or heard or read about), and more rapidly than a Cray Computer you pulled together those similarities and processed the relevant evaluations ("relevant" in whatever way your mind recognized as related to the problem your mind was solving). Amazingly, other human beings, despite the wide variations in all the life experiences that they've had, tend to come to the same conclusions about the sliced-cake variations. This remarkable fact can only be attributed to a deep consensus about justice, a shared sense of justice.

It is remarkable even though few have remarked about it. We take these amazing mental processes for granted largely because there is not much to say about them. We live in a media-heavy language-dominated culture which favors all "reasoning" processes that can be explained and over-explained in terms of words. There is a heavy stock in trade over "reasoned" accounts of things. But when it comes to making justice judgments, the very fact (as I contend) that they are made without language means that they are not going to be written up by the purveyors of reasoning. Our society vastly overrates thinking processes that are "explained" in words (even though words do not and cannot explain them), and undervalues the more remarkable ordinary and everyday judgments that we reach rather effortlessly.[9] Indeed, the very convergence of our conclusions about justice—the fact for example that my forty-four students were unanimous on every aspect and variation of the sliced-cake problem—tends to ensure that few will write about the process. There is no "news value" in repeating what everybody already knows, especially if the process itself is hard to describe.

One does not have to be worldly-wise to share in the consensus about justice outcomes. We can easily imagine little Johnny in the above example knowing right away whether his mother is treating him fairly. If we, like Johnny, were that "good" at assessing justice when we are children, then our sense of justice is only refined with ever increasing sensitivity as we get older and wiser. Perhaps our

[9] Compare the underevaluation our society accords to the "intelligence" that goes into music and art. Few people will admit that Charlie Parker or George Shearing exhibited in music the heights of intellect that Bertrand Russell or Ludwig Wittgenstein exhibited in philosophy.

minds are just superb machines when it comes to remembering and comparing life situations. Our selves just seem to have been constructed that way.

The facts that our minds are able to notice what our minds deem the "relevant" similarities in thousands of diverse situations, and that our minds reach justice conclusions about those situations that cohere with a general consensus of minds, have a feedback effect upon the situations themselves. People in a society tend to act in ways that are generally approved by others. Most mothers, unlike our hypothetical mother, would only give one child a smaller slice of cake if that were the fair thing to do in the judgment of others (including their children) and in their own judgment (which we have found would be similar to the judgment of others). With millions of people reacting to billions of situations, and with their reactions influenced by what they and others regard as the fair or just decision that should be reached in those situations, the situations tend to get restructured coherently. Because people make situations and interact with them, we find that the world is altered so that it more nearly conforms with fairness judgments about those situations. Thus, if Stevie cleaned his room but Johnny didn't, and Johnny wants a slice of cake as big as Stevie's, the mother may tell Johnny that he can have a bigger slice if he promises to clean his room right after dinner. That promise, and Johnny's subsequent fulfillment of the promise, is an example of what I mean by the changes effected in the real world because of a felt need of persons to conform their behavior, and shape the behavior of others, to judgments about justice.

I certainly do not claim that all judgments cohere with the general consensus about justice. Indeed, the first two examples in the cake case illustrate judgments that are distinctly unjust. The world is not a perfect paradigm of enacted justice. There is a considerable amount of injustice "noise" in the vast web of justice communications in the world. However, I suggest that there would be much more noise if courts did not exist.

Despite my claim that millions of people reacting to billions of situations inject a certain amount of justice coherence into social interactions, nevertheless we cannot say that, left to itself, injustice might not "catch on" and flourish in a given society. Disputes might be "resolved" in favor of the physically stronger party or the party who has rounded up enough friends. A social device needs to be invented that leaves justice-oriented actions in place and changes unjust actions to just actions. Hence we need authoritative dispute-resolving mechanisms to convert unjust impulses into just results.

F. JUSTICE AND THE JUDICIAL ROLE

In particular, we need a social device that leaves justice-oriented actions in place and changes unjust actions to just actions. We might consider, from the world of physics, an analogy to such a device. In the nineteenth century, James Clerk Maxwell posited the following situation: A box is divided by a partition into two chambers, A and B, with a small trapdoor in the partition. A tiny being at the trapdoor—"Maxwell's demon"—opens or closes the trapdoor at will. When a fast moving molecule of gas in chamber A is at the trapdoor, the demon opens the door and lets the molecule into chamber B. When a slow-moving molecule from chamber B is near the trapdoor, the demon opens the trapdoor and lets the molecule go into chamber A. As a result, chamber A will eventually have all the slow-moving molecules and B the fast-moving molecules. This means that B will have the higher temperature (heat is defined as the relative degree of motion of molecules). Maxwell's demon would thus have succeeded in violating the second law of thermodynamics, creating an ordered disparity between the two chambers or, in other words, generating negative entropy.[10]

I now suggest that in social systems, courts act out the function of Maxwell's demon. Situations are inputted to courts by way of pleadings; they are processed; the "just" situations are passed through without change (i.e., case dismissed), and the "unjust" ones are corrected by a judgment that is then forcibly implemented. The result is the infusion of negative entropy into society by judicial decisions. The judicial mechanism acts as a regulator or governor by filtering out (reversing, destroying the consequences of) unjust behavior, while leaving in (as Maxwell's demon did) the situations that are already in general conformity with justice (in the demon's

[10] In 1950, Leon Brillouin exorcised the demon by demonstrating that the negative entropy from the demon's action would be exceeded by the increase in entropy needed for the demon's choosing between fast and slow molecules.

case, the nonagitated molecules). In sum, the amount of justice coherence in society is increased by the output of courts and disorder (positive entropy) is reduced.

In the social setting, only a few courts are needed if the society already reflects a considerable amount of coherence. The institutionalization of compulsory adjudication not only results in court decisions that "correct" the disorderly private decisions (the unjust ones), but also—because humans and not inanimate molecules are involved—communicate to the general public a series of lessons about the kinds of activities that are unjust and hence ought to be avoided.

Order and stability of expectations are increased in a society if the court does a good job in weeding out the unjust outcomes and constantly replenishing them with outcomes that comport with justice. People begin structuring their situations to avoid the forcible reversing mechanism of courts. And that is why justice "spreads" through the society. Courts naturally want to contribute to the spread of justice, since courts themselves "thrive" in situations of order and stability. (You only have to imagine anarchy and chaos in a society to see that courts would be swamped with cases. And if the decisions of those courts are unjust, they would simply add to the anarchy instead of straightening it out. Soon the courts would be written off as totally ineffective.)

Deciding cases according to their similarity to previous justice-outcomes (what in the law is simply the operation of "precedent") then becomes the most important guiding mechanism for judges. The mechanism is not inside the judge's head (except in the sense that everything we do proceeds from the way our minds have organized the data). The mechanism is not subjective. Rather, justice is an objective phenomenon. Its effects can be seen in the stability of expectations in a functioning social system. A trial judge who does not have a sense of justice will probably find himself reversed by the appellate court. Reversals will continue until the trial judge learns (through trial-and-error!) how to decide cases justly.

And that is why I think justice plays a major role in the operation of law. We have to take our sense of justice into account in predicting what courts will do. Which is another way of saying that law and justice are not separate concepts but rather are inherently related to each other. If you have worked through this difficult Chapter with me, and if you have expended the mental effort necessary to challenge the Separation Thesis, you are probably well on your way to being a good predictor of the law and a good judge of whether a person's contemplated course of action is legal or illegal.

You might say that everything I've argued for in this book boils down to "common sense." If you say that, I will agree with you emphatically. The main problem with the law as it exists today in an advanced country like the United States is that legalisms and technicalities have gotten in the way of common sense. Some lawyers and some judges have lost sight of common sense and justice because they have been snowed by an avalanche of words. But words should be instruments of mental freedom and not prisons for our thoughts. The word is never important; what counts is the act, the situation, the real lives of real people in the world. "Law" becomes more understandable, and more useful, if it is seen as a justice-correcting mechanism for real events and real situations. Real law, and hopefully not the language of law, has a small but significant role to play in the hopes and dreams of people as we struggle to make sense of our existence on this ecologically frail minor planet.

G. LAW SCHOOLS AND JUSTICE

Now it is time to be critical about the way law is taught in law schools today. My argument is that their emphasis should be on justice and not on "law." Students should learn "law" as a by-product of their law-school investigation into what is just and unjust about our society, our government, our way of life, and what can be done about injustice through the judicial system. If you have not enrolled in a law school but are thinking about doing so, you may not see the relevance of criticizing that which you have not yet experienced. My answer is that a critical attitude toward *everything* is the hallmark of a good lawyer. And so, if you are critical about the educational process itself, not only are you sharpening your legal-analytic ability, but you may get more out of that educational process. Often the engine that powers a change in a law school's curriculum is set in motion by the students and not by the faculty. The following, therefore, is my plea to new students of the law.

There used to be lawyers in the United States well before there were law schools. Young lawyers learned their trade by serving as apprentice to a practicing lawyer. Although we can only revisit in our imaginations the rough features of the apprenticeship model, I think that doing so will give us a benchmark to evaluate what law school education is like today.

We go back a century or two. We start with a young man with a good mind who wants to become a lawyer. (Alas, there were only male lawyers at that time, so I will not be using the pronoun "she.") The young man finds a practicing attorney who is willing to take him on as an apprentice.

Does the attorney give the young man homework reading assignments, ask him questions about the reading on a daily basis, and then periodically administer written examinations—the way law schools do today? Clearly not; the practicing attorney was too busy to engage in that kind of abstract education. Instead, the young man shows up and immediately tries to learn as much as he can while making himself useful to the attorney. He sits with the attorney and takes notes as the latter interviews clients and asks them questions. The young man serves as general clerk and secretary, rewriting in a careful hand Mrs. Smith's will and Mr. Perkins' proposal for a joint venture. Suppose a client has to execute a deed. The attorney might give the young apprentice a book to take home with him that evening, *Deeds on Conveyancing.* The apprentice duly reads and studies the book and attempts to familiarize himself with the existing law on conveyancing as summarized by Deeds. The next day he shows up bright and early at the firm, and learns that much of what he read in the book is unnecessary and misleading—although not all of it. "The way we handle conveyances in this firm," says the attorney, "differs in important respects from what you can find in books. I want you to read the books to get a general view, but read them with a skeptical eye. Then come in and learn how it's really done."

The apprentice accompanies the attorney at a meeting of the town's governing body. The apprentice learns first hand the way legal advice is given to political bodies. He gets to know the important leaders in the town. He sits at the attorney's side in meetings of company boards of directors.

Sometimes the apprentice has to copy over a brief written by the attorney. The copying process helps him become familiar with the issues in the brief. As he learns more about how law is practiced, he makes suggestions—"here is one of the cases you asked me to read last night that I think we should cite in the brief," or "I thought of an argument that the other side might make." He attends negotiations and courtroom trials, and learns by observation and limited participation how the attorney operates.

If we try to characterize the "message" that the apprentice receives about the practice of law, it might go something as follows: *an attorney tries first of all to help people avoid problems or, if necessary, to help them deal with problems that have arisen.* This characterization—implicit or explicit in everything the attorney does during the day—tells the apprentice the *what* of the law. As his apprenticeship proceeds he increasingly learns the *how* of the law. Another message he absorbs with time is the *why* of the law. For the mere avoidance or solution of problems is not enough to make law a *profession.* Surely, one could be skeptical about the mere desirability of avoiding problems—perhaps avoiding them is a bad idea, resulting in a more boring life. Thus, if the apprentice were to ask the lawyer the *why* question, the lawyer might respond: "*an attorney tries, in his limited way, to promote justice.* If a client comes in with a fraudulent scheme in mind, like Mr. Johnstone the other day, you noticed I tried to talk him out of it. If a client wants to take unfair advantage of another person, I try to show him the disadvantages of that course of action—and I don't shy away from telling him that it is not morally right, if he'll listen to that line of argument. I certainly try to tell him why the course of action may backfire on him. But also, as you've noticed, if a client comes in with a just cause—if our client the Presbyterian church has been swindled, or if Mrs. Thompson has been hurt by a carriage that was negligently manufactured—then it is our job to obtain redress for our clients in whatever official forums are available. *Even if the law seems to be stacked against clients who have a just cause, we have to figure out a way to turn it around and make the law work for them.*"

I am not trying to paint a Polyannish picture of the past. There may indeed have been attorneys whose goal was to acquire wealth by telling clients how to commit fraud. Rather, I am attempting to reconstruct what an attorney might say to his apprentice that would have appealed to the apprentice's sense about why the practice of law is morally worthwhile. If the apprentice decided to become a lawyer because he felt that he wanted to be part of a noble profession—because he wanted to do some good in the world before passing on—then the lawyer's statement may have been close to what lawyers actually used to say. Recall that in the United States at the time of the adoption of the Constitution, lawyering was regarded as a noble profession. Indeed, it was lawyers who wrote the Constitution.

The most important aspect so far of my picture of the apprenticeship system is what was not said. The lawyer in my example said very little about *law.* The "content of the law" is only of secondary importance in the master attorney's daily practice; what is important is people and their problems. "Law" is just a set of tools that can be utilized to help people avoid or solve their problems. Yet, I shall contend that the "law" that is left *out* of my account of the apprenticeship system is mostly what is put *in* to legal education. And that at bottom is what can be distorting and soulless about legal education.

To the busy practicing attorney, law is nothing more than a set of tools. She does not devote excessive time to the study of these tools. Rather, she is in the "people business," the "problem-avoiding" business, the "problem solving" business, and the "justice" business. Her day is full of these concerns. She does not study "the law" in general, and only "keeps up" with legal developments that are very close to the areas of her practice. Helping people avoid problems, or solve the problems that come up, helps achieve overall justice. Achieving overall justice is not only *good for business* (the lawyer's reputation for probity in the community will redound to her financial success), but indeed constitutes the reason why the *practice* of law can be morally self-fulfilling.

Since the point I am making—that law is simply a tool and not an end in itself—is so critical here, allow me one other analogy to days of old. Consider an apprentice to a master carpenter. The master carpenter does not spend more than the briefest amount of time introducing the apprentice to the tools of the trade. He doesn't quiz his apprentice on the theory of different kinds of sandpaper. Instead, the carpenter says, "here, rub this No. 3 sandpaper this way, with the grain of the wood, but keep checking it against the light to see that it is flat." The apprentice completes the task, and the master carpenter says, "now you want a finer finish. So look for some sandpaper with finer sand on it." The apprentice thus learns the actual uses of sandpaper, as well as how to use the file and the plane to put a smooth finish on the wood. He learns the uses of these and other tools all for the purpose of helping the master craftsman turn out actual pieces of furniture. The "best" tool for a particular job is primarily a function of what the job ought to be, and secondarily a function of what tools are available. It is in the conceptualization of the job that the apprentice learns how to become a master craftsman. A particular table, for example, is being designed for Mrs. Field's living room. She is tall, so the table must be higher than average. She wants a drawer under the tabletop for papers, and wants to be able to sit at the table (thus the legs of the table have to be free-standing and not reinforced by cross bars). Oak would be the best color for the living room, but oak is one of the hardest of woods and so the construction of this table will take twice as long as normal—this has to be figured into the estimated price. Most important of all, the table has to be aesthetically pleasing. It is almost impossible to teach the apprentice aesthetics, but hopefully the apprentice will show an aptitude for it (and if not, the apprentice will probably not become a master craftsman). If the apprentice has an innate sense of aesthetics, then the most important thing he can learn from the master craftsman is how to make fine judgments between this alternative and that one (what this piece of wood will look like, when stained, and how strong it is compared to that wood, and whether existing tools can be effectively utilized to achieve the final "look" that is desired).

Neither for the law apprentice nor for the carpenter apprentice are the tools the important thing. To focus excessively on the tools would be to distort the mental processes of judgment that must be brought to bear in the successful discharge of the profession. The apprentice carpenter soon discovers, for example, what can best be done with a plane and what can best be done with sandpaper, but he also discovers that if one isn't available you can get along fairly well, although less efficiently, with the other. But it is not by studying sandpaper that he becomes a master craftsman. Rather, it is by studying the problems that people have (Mrs. Field wants a nice looking, serviceable table), and the goals he wants to achieve on their behalf (she will be pleased if he presents her with an aesthetically pleasing yet durable and functional table), that he can look forward to a successful and satisfying career as a master craftsman. Mrs. Field is only interested in the resulting table; she has no direct interest (though she may be interested for other reasons) in the tools that were used to do the work.

Professions and crafts are properly judged by the results they produce, and not by the techniques that are brought to bear in producing those results. Yet we see in many aspects of present-day life examples of runaway technique. Consider the pianist at a piano bar in a restaurant or night club who has a dazzling technique, but who produces boring music. Keyboard virtuosity is no substitute for "soul"—for the kind of musical ability that understands what moods and ideas the composer was trying to achieve and how to read and interpret the composer's score to recapture those emotions. We see student editors publishing law review articles apparently on the sole basis of the impressiveness of the lengthy footnotes—for footnotes are but the trappings and not the substance of scholarship. We purchase technologically sophisticated word-processing systems only to discover that the instruction manuals are incomprehensible, incoherent, and disorganized. The manuals exhibit no sense of what a typical user wants the software to do. Rather, the manuals want to tell us all at once everything that the software itself can do—a glorification of technique over substance. When, many years ago, the legal apprentice system was gradually replaced by law schools, what happened was that students were taught "the law" in abstraction. To be sure, "cases" were read, but the facts of those cases were taken as stated by the courts (which present a highly selective and often misleading picture of the actual facts). In contrast, the apprentice had learned the facts of cases by daily contact with clients. Students in law school get only a truncated and highly selected version of the facts. Moreover, law schools considered it to be entirely irrelevant what happened to the parties after the case was handed down (did they settle? Did they continue to litigate? Was the judgment ever paid? What effect did the case have on their lives?) In contrast, the young apprentice lawyer had to live with the effects of his legal work on his clients. He had to "follow through" in the lives of his clients, not only because he was dependent upon them for his livelihood but because any legal work he did for them was only part of their general situation. No case was "discrete"; nearly everything about the practice of law was relational.

Perhaps the first thing that went wrong with law schools was giving them the *name* "law school." (Things might have turned out differently had they been called colleges of justice.) The name "law school" gave rise to an expectation that this was a school to which a person could go to "learn the law." At that point, self-defined academic concerns began to reconceptualize what "learning the law" meant. Professors began to write textbooks on what "the law" consisted of, and to sell these books to their students as required reading. To ensure that the students read the books, the professors quizzed the students on their ability to regurgitate the rules contained in the texts. Students "fought back" by inventing the law review, where they could accept or reject professorial essays. A revolution of sorts was accomplished by Christopher Columbus Langdell at the end of the nineteenth century. He called for the replacement of textbooks by appellate court opinions. Since this took a source of publication (of texts) away from the law faculty, they countered by compiling casebooks of cases and excerpts from appellate court decisions. New texts—hornbooks and nutshells—were written to explain to the lazy student what the cases meant. Finally, today, casebooks and texts are merging. We are seeing more and more editorial notes and comments in "casebooks," and less and less of cases. What cases are given are severely truncated, and—what is the worst development of all—the "facts" are often omitted.

Law schools occasioned an explosion of legal writing. Every published essay potentially gave birth to a host of competing, critical essays. Much of the writing concerned the interpretation of legal texts and the theories that could be invented and used to construe those texts. Theories spawned more theories. At the present time, to exaggerate only slightly, a single case or statute is significant only because it instantiates—or in the alternative repudiates—Hobbes, Hegel, Hume, Habermas, Heidegger, Heisenberg, Hayek, or hermeneutics.

Instead of learning through the apprenticeship system that law was a set of tools whose function was to help people avoid or solve problems in the interests of societal justice, students began to be examined on their mastery of the content of the tools themselves. The result was, and has been, a wrenching distortion of what law is all about. Yet I must make it clear that I am not advocating a return to the apprenticeship system. Law schools historically have played the immensely important role of destroying the "old boy" network of legal apprenticeship, opening the legal profession to all persons. We are a much more egalitarian society as a result of the law-school movement. Nor am I necessarily advocating an expansion of "clinical education" in law schools or the "legal skills" movement, though these are important. My criticism of law school education is not over techniques of teaching but rather is about the fact that justice seems to have receded into the background.

Where can we find justice in the casebooks that law students read? An average casebook gives a condensed summary of the facts of cases—condensed by the editors from the court's own opinion, which itself was already a highly selective and summarized account of the facts. The casebook then goes on to present portions of the court's reasoning. What we need to know most of all are the facts that are missing. What were the real facts of the case? What stories did the parties tell their attorneys? What did the attorneys do with those stories? Did the attorneys advise the parties to take further steps either to improve their eventual litigating position or to avoid litigation entirely? What was that advice? Did the clients take it? Was it good advice? When the case got to trial, what did the jury hear? What can we find in the transcript of the trial? What about evidence that the jury did not hear, because the judge ruled that it was inadmissible? How did the attorneys argue the inadmissibility questions? What were the attorneys' final statements to the jury? All of these questions arise before the appellate court ever gets the case and before the appellate court summarizes the facts. We need to know the answers to some of these questions, at least, before we can determine whether the appellate court's summary of the facts is fair and accurate. Furthermore, there are factual questions that arise *after* the appellate court has ruled. Was the judgment ever collected? Was the case settled after the court's ruling came in? If it was a criminal case, what happened to the defendant? If the defendant was later pardoned by the governor on the ground of innocence, should not that fact alone cast doubt on the fairness of the court's proceeding? Finally, what role did the judgment play in the lives of the parties? Did both sides accept the judgment and move on with their lives, or was one side permanently embittered by the judgment? In commercial cases, what steps were taken by the losing party to change its ways of doing business? If the losing party regarded the judicial decision as unjust, what steps if any did it take to retaliate against the winner?

Of course, I exaggerate. Some law schools do the "justice" job a lot better than others. Yet I fear that a majority of law professors today would say that whatever happened to the parties before the case or after the case—things the court did not know about or mention—have absolutely nothing to do with the law.

But it is precisely this notion of irrelevance that I am attacking. *Why* are the questions of what really happened to the parties *irrelevant?* That they may appear to be *legally irrelevant* under the law as we presently conceive it says nothing about what the law ought to be. Maybe it only suggests how myopic our present view of "law" really is. Law as presently conceived wears blinders that block out observation of what happens to real people in real situations. Yet what happens to real people in real situations is what justice is all about. Thus it is our present notion of "law" that needs rethinking. For "law" is and can be only the existential appearance of words printed on paper. Changes in those texts are perhaps curious phenomena, worthy of an arcane scholar's inquiry (although our law reviews are full of such endeavors). But in every case that our students will ever be called upon to handle in real life, the words on the law-book pages have no intrinsic interest—they are simply the Given. The attorney is called upon to take what is Given and show the court that a proper, fair, reasonable, and just interpretation of the Given is necessary in order to do justice to the parties. The opposing attorneys will disagree as to what interpretation is proper, fair, reasonable, and just. And the question will be settled—assuming a fair-minded judge interested in doing justice—according to a comparative evaluation of the *facts* as presented by both sides against the judge's sense of justice. The "facts" cannot be legally circumscribed without falling back into the regressive view of "law" that I am attacking. Rather, it is the inherent empathetic appreciation of the facts that should drive our interpretation of the "relevant" legal rules. To do it the other way round—to say that the legal rules *tell us* what facts are relevant—is to put on legal blinders (blinders of our own making) and thus perpetuate injustice and bad lawyering.

If law schools focus on justice and not on "law," they will discover, I believe, that their students will get a better *legal* training than they now get! How would justice-teaching work? The ideal classroom exercise would go beyond the case to inquire whether there might have been other facts that the attorneys might have adduced that could have shifted the justice considerations to the other side. What kinds of facts might they have been? Do we have any evidence that they were in fact available to the attorneys? Were important justice-facts excluded at the trial for evidentiary or strategic reasons? And are *we* unintentionally excluding a set of relevant facts because they seem to come under the aegis of some law-school course other than the present course?

Indeed, the "justice dialogue"—whether in the classroom or among a group of friends conversing socially—invariably consists of adducing more facts and arguing for their analogical relevance. To revert to the cake-dividing example in Section E of this Chapter, some of the mother's explanations for giving the larger slice to Steve seem to call out for additional facts. When she answers, "Because it's Tuesday," we need to know more. Is she alternating between her two children depending on the day of the week? Is there some other form of compensation for Johnny (who on Tuesday is getting the smaller slice?) A classroom discussion of a case can elicit questions as to the sort of facts that might make a justice-difference to the decision maker. Some of these facts might be available in the court's own summary of the facts; others might be provided by the casebook editor; and still others would be speculative. A search for justice-facts is what the first interview between an attorney and a prospective client is all about. The attorney is not content just to listen to the client's story; rather, questions and follow-up questions are asked in order to get the kind of factual picture that the attorney can then examine to see whether there is any cost-effective recourse for the client that the lawyer can provide.

The justice-dialogue in the classroom may or may not lead to a conclusion that one side is "right" and the other is "wrong." But this conclusion will be debated, and the debate will focus primarily on the competing stories of the clients, fleshed out by the further elucidation of facts (or hypothetical facts) resulting from the classroom discussion. Legal *theories* serve as a *heuristic* in the minds of students who are elucidating these further facts. But the theories are not themselves the end of the story—any theory overdetermines the facts and any set of facts underdetermines the theory. What finally counts, when heuristics are exhausted, is the sense of justice that one party's story is more morally compelling than the other's.

Can such justice-dialogues be *taught?* Obviously yes, although what is required is classroom dialogue. Lecturing does not work here. (Indeed, lecturing does not even work well for traditional law instruction.) Nor can any textbook do the justice job. There is no lecture or textual substitute for teaching justice in the classroom. In one sense, my argument for teaching justice in law schools is a return to the value of civilized dialogue. This value is largely being lost in a media-hyped age. When we actually have the luxury of a classroom dialogue, it is a sheer waste for the professor to deliver a lecture. For a lecture can be written and distributed to the students to read at their own leisure (i.e., when they are watching television). It cannot do the justice job, which is a conversation job.

The classroom dialogue is enhanced because students know the actual result that was reached by the court. They can then ask whether the court reached a just result. If unjust, what did the parties do (or what could they have done?) after the judgment was rendered in order to ameliorate the injustice? What steps could either party take in the future to change their behavior in order to live with the result reached by the court?

The "analytical skills" law schools teach would not be all that different if their focus is on justice. Students will still receive the same basic, and I think excellent, law-school training in analysis, organization, and persuasion. But I think the students' level of interest will be much higher because the exercises are conducted with a purpose—a human purpose, the purpose of discovering more and more about justice and how fair solutions to problems can help people live better and more satisfying lives (including lives that are not wrenched and distorted by the intrusion of law and litigation).

But it is quite clear that the analytical questions that professors would ask when justice and not law is the focus of the classroom exercise, will be more factual. Law-questions tend to pile theory upon theory, rationalization upon rationalization, invented category upon invented category. These may be intellectually stimulating exercises, but they have little to do with influencing the decisions that judges make. In contrast, justice-questions will be more factual—we need more and more evidence of what people did, what they did not do (perhaps on advice of counsel), and what happened to them when they acted or avoided acting. It should be the facts that drive the theory (including the theory that the case at hand is a Contracts case and not a Torts case, or the other way round).

Teaching from a justice perspective does not mean that a case will be analyzed from one side only. Law schools can and should teach both sides of the case, not only because practicing attorneys must be prepared to argue for their clients regardless of what side of a case their clients are on, but also because it is necessary in preparing one side of a case to *imagine* what the best arguments are on the other side of the case. Teaching from a justice perspective means looking at both sides of the case critically and coming to a conclusion that, on the facts as given, one side has the better claim in justice than the other side. Moreover, one of the most important "justice" lessons that can be learned is the "ability to put yourself in the other person's shoes," or what Hume called "sympathy" and what we now call "empathy." Putting yourself in another person's shoes requires knowing a lot more about that person and the facts of that person's situation than simply knowing the content of law-words. Thus teaching from a justice perspective can significantly improve empathic argumentative ability—something which law schools are already doing fairly well.

In sum, excessive preoccupation with the tools (the law-words) of the legal system distorts, in some students' minds perhaps irrevocably, what law is all about and what it is for. It elevates tools over goals, form over substance, manipulations over justice.

If law schools make a greater effort teach their students that what matters is justice, sooner or later society will learn the same thing. Law graduates will eventually fill the benches of the courts throughout the country. What *they* think the law is will be what the law will become. If law schools succeed in broadening their conceptions of "law" when they are in law school, sooner or later that same conception will *define* what law is and will then be accepted as ordinary. Ultimately, everyone should perceive that justice is what law is all about.

H. ADVOCACY AND JUSTICE

Justice is what law is for; justice is what judges should render; justice is what lawyers should achieve. Law without justice is nothing but a set of tools, incapable of solving human problems. Like any tool, law may facilitate the solution of a given problem—although misconceived laws may create more problems than they solve. If legal education did nothing more than train students in how to find and use the tools of the trade, then that education would hardly be ennobling, would hardly bestow upon lawyering the label of "profession," would hardly account for students' decisions to become lawyers. Nor can lawyers fall back on the position that their only duty is to serve their clients, because some things that clients want done should not be done (such as planning a crime). It is the professional responsibility of lawyers to stop clients from doing such things. If serving a client is a lawyer's highest aspiration, then that lawyer is just a hired gun. To the contrary, the reason law is properly called a profession is because its purpose is to help achieve justice—justice for clients, to be sure, but justice nevertheless. By achieving justice for clients, lawyers add a measure of justice to society. The more that justice is meted out to individuals, the more society will become a just society. Louis Brandeis once said that a lawyer's duty is not to his client, but to his client's situation. That has always seemed to me to be a profound observation, yet I venture to suggest that it could be modified: a lawyer's duty is to the justice within a client's situation.

APPENDIX. FURTHER DEVELOPMENT OF THE ECONOMIC ARGUMENT CONTAINED IN CHAPTER 2

TO WHOM DOES THE LAW ASSIGN THE ENTITLEMENT?

We've been examining the question whether the homeowners near the proposed factory have a property entitlement or a liability entitlement to clean air. But the law doesn't necessarily have to give the homeowners any entitlement at all. What if the law gave the entitlement instead to the factory? Suppose a sovereign entity, such as a state or a nation, simply decides to industrialize as rapidly as possible, and thus assigns all entitlements to business enterprises. By asking these questions and testing their implications, we can get a more complete picture of the way that legal entitlements work.

We'll assume that the legislature decides to award a property entitlement to all industries who pollute the air. As we have seen, this would mean that a cement factory would have a right to pollute the air without compensating anyone. What would be the consequence?

Suppose the people in a town don't want the factory to locate there. But the factory has a property entitlement to pollute the air. Assume the factory purchases a vacant piece of property and announces its construction plans. The nearby homeowners form a committee to talk to the factory's management. "How can we stop you from building a factory in our fair town?" they ask.

We're not unreasonable people," management replies. "We only want to build a factory in this town because we project a 12% return on our invested capital. We could go to another town, but that would only give us a return of 11%."

The homeowners then say, "if you sell us the property you bought, plus the air pollution entitlement, we'll give you your original price of the land back, plus enough profit so that you can go to the next town and buy land with the profit we've given you. In that way, your investment costs in the next town will be substantially lower than they are here, and you can make better than a 12% return on your money there."

If management accepts this deal, the homeowners will have purchased the vacant piece of property from the factory plus all the property entitlements that go with it. Then, presumably, they will build a park there, or attract some light non-polluting industry.

But there's a hitch. Recall that when the shoe was on the other foot—when the townspeople had a property entitlement in clean air—it was next to impossible for the factory to buy up every homeowner's entitlement because of the high transaction costs including the problem of "holdouts." Now the townspeople, through their committee, want to purchase the property entitlement to pollute from the factory. But how will they raise the necessary money from all the homeowners? Won't some homeowners say to themselves, "let them raise the money from all my neighbors, and then when they come to me, I'll stall them and keep stalling them and never pay my share. They'll be so close to having raised the necessary money that they'll each throw in a little bit more and make up my share for me. In that way, I'll benefit from the cement factory not being built, but I won't have to pay for it."

This is the classic "free rider" problem. It is the converse of the "holdout" problem. It comes up in many community situations. Suppose the neighbors of a nuclear power plant want to raise money to bring a lawsuit. They go from door to door, asking for contributions. Some people—often many—will turn them down, expecting to benefit as free riders from the contributions of everyone else.

We're beginning to see that it's just as hard for the factory, in the original case, to buy up all the property entitlements from the neighbors, as it is in the case we've just discussed for the neighbors to chip in to buy the property entitlement from the factory. We can tentatively conclude that, in matters of zoning and clean air and industrial development, "property entitlements" are cumbersome instruments. When a progressive society wants to deal flexibly with economic matters, the law is more likely to favor liability entitlements over property entitlements.

So let's investigate what would happen if we give the liability entitlement to the factory. Recall that when I first discussed liability entitlements, we assumed that the law gave the townspeople a liability entitlement to clean air. But now let us consider what would happen if the law gives the cement factory a liability entitlement to pollute the air.

We again assume that a corporation has purchased some vacant land in the town and announces its plans to build a cement factory. Its liability entitlement gives it the legal right to pollute the air. However, because it is a liability entitlement and not a property entitlement, the plant can be forced to sell the entitlement at an objectively reasonable price.

So, we imagine that the people convene in town hall and pass a zoning ordinance taking away the company's liability entitlement to pollute the air. The town will then have to compensate the company. The amount of compensation might be considerable, since the factory purchased the vacant land with the plan to build a cement factory that would be very profitable. Once the town takes away the liability entitlement, the factory cannot be built. The company has lost something of value, and must receive reasonable compensation. The amount of the compensation would be computed as the amount the investment value of the land is reduced considering that polluting factories no longer can be built on the land.

If the town goes ahead and takes away the factory's liability entitlement, the town can raise the money to pay the factory simply by taxing the people of the town—such as by increasing the real estate tax. This avoids the free rider problem.

ECONOMIC DETERMINISM

To whom *should* the law assign the entitlements? To the townspeople or to the factory? What difference would it make?

If you are a homeowner and the law has assigned clean-air entitlements to you, then your house is more valuable than it would be without those entitlements. You can sell your clean-air entitlements to new industries who want to move into town. On the other hand, if the law has assigned the entitlements to the factory, then the factory can go ahead and pollute your air and you won't be compensated for the pollution.

So having entitlements clearly makes a difference in terms of *comparative wealth.* You're richer if you have various entitlements, and you're poorer if you don't have them.

But does the assignment of entitlements make any difference in terms of whether a cement factory will move into a particular town? Suppose you hear in your hometown that there are plans to erect a factory near your house. And suppose further that your town council had the free choice of deciding whether to grant a clean-air liability entitlement to the townspeople or to the prospective factory. If you went to the town meeting and argued that the factory must be kept out, could you demonstrate that the way to do it is to assign the clean-air liability entitlement to the residents of the town and not to the factory?

The economist Ronald Coase in 1960 answered this general question in a startling fashion. Coase proved that whether the law gives clean-air entitlements to the townspeople or polluted-air entitlements to the factory makes no difference. The factory's decision to come into the town, or to stay out, will not be affected by the assignment of entitlements.

We have to be clear that Coase is not saying that it makes no difference to the factory itself or to the townspeople themselves what the liability entitlement is. If the people have a liability entitlement in clean air, then the factory will have to pay each of them money when the court decides what those clean air entitlements are worth. On the other hand, if the factory has a liability entitlement to pollute, then it will receive money from the people who want to avoid the pollution. In one case the people end up with more money, in the other, the factory ends up with more money. That result is what we all would expect; after all, if you have rights, you can sell them; if you don't have them, you don't have anything to sell. So whether you end up with extra money or you have to pay depends upon the way the law makes the initial assignment of liability entitlements. The question of relative wealth is important, but it's not the question Coase addressed.

Coase's theorem is that whether or not the cement factory will ultimately be built in the town is independent of the question of whether the law gives to the townspeople or to the factory the liability entitlements. Can you see why?

Here's a way of working through the Coase theorem. Let's say that an objectively determined valuation of clean air in a given town is $5 million. The $5 million represents the value of the difference to all the townspeople of clean air versus air that would be polluted from the factory to be built on the cement company's land. Now suppose further that the cement company figures the costs of construction of the factory to be $40 million. The company further calculates that it can make a reasonable return on its investment if the total cost of the factory is $50 million or less. Since its construction cost would be $40 million, it figures it can afford to spend up to $10 million for purchasing air entitlements.

Now let's consider two cases: in Case I, the law gives the clean-air liability entitlement to the townspeople. In that case, the factory will be built, and the company will pay $5 million to the townspeople as the objective value of their liability entitlement to clean air. The company will be glad to pay the $5 million and will go ahead and build the cement factory, because its total cost would be $45 million, which is less than its top economically feasible cost of $50 million.

Now consider Case II, where the law gives the liability entitlement to the company to pollute the air. Then, as we have previously seen, the townspeople would want to condemn those rights by eminent domain proceedings, but the most they would be willing to pay the company would be $5 million. Any higher amount, and the townspeople would prefer the polluted air. You can see this if you imagine yourself to be one of the homeowners in the town. You're willing to pay your individual assessment of $1,000 to the factory to purchase their pollution rights, but any more than that and you say, forget it, I won't pay anything and I'll accept the polluted air. So the total amount the townspeople as a whole are willing to pay the company not to build the factory is $5 million.

But will the factory accept $5 million for its entitlement? We've seen that the worth of the pollution rights to the company is $10 million—which is the amount the factory would pay, if it had to, to proceed with the cement business. In other words—and this is the economically critical point—it's worth up to $10 million for the factory to go ahead with the cement business, but only worth up to $5 million for the townspeople to stop the factory. The factory can demonstrate in court, if it has to, that its entitlement to pollute the air is worth $10 million to it, even though the townspeople are only offering $5 for the entitlement. Since the economic worth of the entitlement to the factory is $10 million, it would have to be compensated $10 million if that entitlement were taken away. But since the town is not willing to go higher than $5 million, the factory will be built.

So we see that the result of Case II is exactly the same as the result of Case I. In both cases, the factory will be built. The assignment of entitlements did not make a difference.

But we can't consider the Coase theorem as proved until we see what would happen if it is not economically feasible for the factory to be built in your town. We should do this by comparing outcomes in two cases where the liability entitlements are assigned differently. But we'll have to use some different numbers to indicate why the cement factory project is *not* feasible in this new instance.

We'll keep the construction cost of $40 million, and retain as well the objectively determined worth of the clean-air rights to the townspeople at $5 million. The difference comes in with the corporation's economists who look at the total cost of the cement factory and estimate how much they can spend to obtain a reasonable return on investment. This time they say that the total cost of the factory cannot exceed $43 million. Any more than that, and the factory isn't an economical proposition for the shareholders of the corporation.

In our new Case III, the liability entitlement is assigned by the law to the townspeople. So the townspeople want no less than $5 million from the factory in payment for their liability entitlement to clean air. But if the company were to pay $5 million, the company would exceed the maximum investment that its own economists say is economically feasible. And so the company will not be able to afford paying $5 million to the townspeople. Hence the townspeople will not sell their liability entitlement to the cement company, and as a result the factory will not be built in that town.

To finish the analysis, we have Case IV in which the law gives the cement company a liability entitlement to pollute the air. The entitlement is now only worth $3 million to the cement company. But the townspeople are willing to pay up to $5 million to purchase the liability entitlement from the company. We know from our earliest experiences with the mercantile world that when a seller has something that is worth 3 cents to him, and a buyer is willing to pay up to 5 cents for that item, the sale will go through. Thus, the townspeople will be able to purchase the liability entitlement from the factory. The company will take that money and use it to invest in a cement factory in a different town. But as far as your town is concerned, the result of Case IV is that the factory will not be built. And that is the same as the result we've reached in Case III.

In sum:

	Liability Entitlement Assigned to	RESULT
Case I	Townspeople	Factory comes in
Case II	Factory	Factory comes in
Case III	Townspeople	Factory stays out
Case IV	Factory	Factory stays out

Surprising as it may seem, whether the factory comes in to town or stays out has nothing to do with whether or not the law gives the people the right to clean air!

In a way, this seems like economic determinism. The "logic" of economics determines where factories will be built and where industrial-free communities will be found.

But in fact it is the opposite of Marxian economic determinism. The Marxists say that the capitalist economy determines what the law will be. The law, according to Marx, reflects the class interests of the bourgeoisie.

Coase is saying, to the contrary, that the law doesn't matter. Instead of being a powerful tool of the rich, the law turns out to have little or no impact upon fundamental economic allocations.[1] Marx thought that factories exploit the proletariat. The Coase theorem—foreshadowed in the writings of the economist A.C. Pigou—shows that factories will be built where people value them more than they value various alternatives (such as clean air). If people place such a value on factories that they prefer them to other alternatives, one can hardly agree with Marx that the factories exploit the people.[2]

But we should not forget that Coase's theorem is a limited one. It only tells us about the decisions that the factories will make. It does not tell us about the wealth consequences of the assignment of entitlements. Whether the townspeople end up with money in their pockets, or whether that money instead will end up in the pockets of the shareholders of the cement company, is indeed a function of the law's distribution of entitlements.

[1] Suppose in the four cases we've analyzed we were dealing with property entitlements instead of liability entitlements. Under Coase's theorem, the results would still be the same. But the analysis would be far more complicated, due to the high transaction costs, and the "holdout" and "free rider" problems.

[2] Of course, particular factories that Marx studied in England had working conditions that today we regard as clearly exploitive. But factories in general do not necessarily exploit workers. Even the exploiting factories that Marx studied were sufficiently attractive to cause an enormous population drain from the countryside into the industrialized cities. Bad as the working conditions looked to Marx (and to us as he reports them), apparently huge numbers of people regarded those conditions and salaries better than working conditions and wages on the farms.

SUGGESTIONS FOR FURTHER READING

The first and in some ways still the best description of rights, duties, powers, privileges, and immunities is Hohfeld, "Some Fundamental Legal Conceptions as Applied in Judicial Reasoning," 23 *Yale Law Journal* 16 (1913); 26 *Yale Law Journal* 710 (1917). You will find, however, that I have departed in significant ways from the Hohfeldian analysis.

For more on the problem of failure to rescue, see Chapter 11 in Anthony D'Amato, *Jurisprudence: A Descriptive and Normative Analysis of Law* 287 (1984).

The path-breaking article on entitlements is by Guido Calabresi & A. Douglas Melamed, "Property Rules, Liability Rules, and Inalienability: One View of the Cathedral," 85 *Harvard Law Review* 1089 (1972). The authors give a more detailed presentation than was possible in the present book.

The seminal article referred to in the concluding section of Chapter 2 is Ronald Coase's, "The Problem of Social Cost," 3 *Journal of Law & Economics* 1 (1960).

The best book on positivism is H.L.A. Hart's, *The Concept of Law* (1961). It should be read carefully and with considerable skepticism.

Hans Kelsen's theories are found primarily in two books: Hans Kelsen, *The Pure Theory of Law* (1967), and Hans Kelsen, *General Theory of Law and State* (1945). Though the former was intended to be the more "popular" version, I've found the latter more accessible and readable.

Further analysis of the theories of Bentham, Austin, and Hart as they relate to the legislature-court problem can be found in Chapter 4 of Anthony D'Amato, *Jurisprudence: A Descriptive and Normative Analysis of Law* 115 (1984).

For the leading philosophical analysis of the interpretation of a speaker's meaning, see Ludwig Wittgenstein, *Philosophical Investigations* (1953).

As fresh and stimulating as the day it was written is Oliver Wendell Holmes', *The Common Law* (1881).

For more on subjective probability, the prediction theory of law, and legal realism, see Chapter 1 of Anthony D'Amato, *Jurisprudence: A Descriptive and Normative Analysis of Law* 5 (1984).

I have presented in greater detail my position on justice in Anthony D'Amato, "On the Connection Between Law and Justice," 26 *Univ. California at Davis Law Review* 527 (1993), reprinted in part in *Philosophy of Law* 19–30 (Joel Feinberg & Hyman Gros, eds., 5th ed. 1995).

Either one of two books by Professor Fuller would give an excellent further account of natural law: Lon L. Fuller, *Anatomy of the Law* (1969); Lon L. Fuller, *The Morality of Law* (rev. ed. 1969). However, the book that influenced me the most was Lon L. Fuller, *The Law In Quest of Itself* (1940), which is the published version of a series of three lectures he delivered to the students of Northwestern Law School in 1940.

And if you like what I've said about common sense and common law, you should read the very best book that has ever been written on the common law, Richard A. Epstein, *Simple Rules for a Complex World* (1995).

INDEX

BY THE SAME AUTHOR

Analytic Jurisprudence Anthology
International Intellectual Property Anthology (with Doris Estelle Long)
International Environmental Law Anthology (with Kirsten Engel)
International Law and Political Reality: Collected Papers Volume One
International Law Coursebook
International Law Anthology
Justice and the Legal System (with Arthur Jacobson)
International Law: Process and Prospect
Jurisprudence: A Descriptive and Normative Analysis of Law
Assyrian Case for Autonomy
International Law and World Order (with Weston & Falk)
Basic Documents in International Law and World Order (with Weston & Falk)
Desegregation from Brown to Alexander: An Exploration of Supreme Court Strategies (with Wasby & Metrailer)
Environment and the Law of the Sea (with John Hargrove)
The Judiciary and Vietnam (with Robert O'Neil)
The Concept of Custom in International Law
The Realities of Vietnam (with Christopher Beal)
The Legality of the Use of Force Short of War (with Robert von Mehren)